2015 Revision
of CSET Math III
Study Guide:
Calculus

Copyright 2015 by Christopher Goff

University of the Pacific

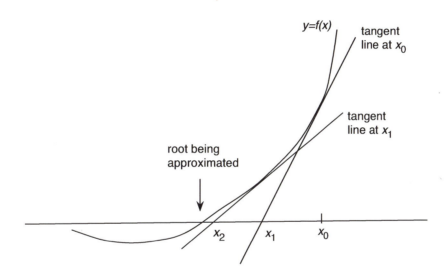

Domains Covered:

5.1 Trigonometry

a. Prove that the Pythagorean Theorem is equivalent to the trigonometric identity $\sin^2 x + \cos^2 x = 1$ **and that this identity leads to** $1 + \tan^2 x = \sec^2 x$ **and** $1 + \cot^2 x = \csc^2 x$

1. What are the six basic trigonometric ratios?

   The six basic trigonometric ratios are sine, cosine, tangent, cotangent, secant, and cosecant. Actually, the "co-" prefix is an abbreviation of "complement's." So, "cosine" means the "complement's sine," that is, the sine of the complementary angle. Use this to complete the following figure.

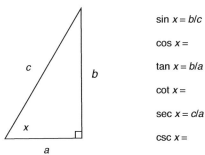

   $\sin x = b/c$

   $\cos x =$

   $\tan x = b/a$

   $\cot x =$

   $\sec x = c/a$

   $\csc x =$

   ANS: $\cos x = \frac{a}{c}$, $\cot x = \frac{a}{b}$, $\csc x = \frac{c}{b}$. From these ratios, it follows that

   $$\tan x = \frac{\sin x}{\cos x}, \quad \cot x = \frac{\cos x}{\sin x}, \quad \sec x = \frac{1}{\cos x}, \quad \text{and} \quad \csc x = \frac{1}{\sin x}.$$

2. Sample Problems

   (a) Draw and label a right triangle with an acute angle x. Write down the Pythagorean Theorem. Divide both sides of the equation by c^2, where c is the hypotenuse length. What do you obtain, in terms of trigonometric functions of x?

   (b) Now divide both sides of the Pythagorean Theorem by a^2, where a is one of the legs. What do you obtain, in terms of trigonometric functions of x?

   (c) Deduce the third Pythagorean Identity. How did you do it?

   (d) One consequence of this standard is that any of these three trigonometric equations is equivalent to any other one. How can you transform $1 + \tan^2 x = \sec^2 x$ into $\sin^2 x + \cos^2 x = 1$ in one step?

3. Answers to Sample Problems

   (a) Draw and label a right triangle with an acute angle x. Write down the Pythagorean Theorem. Divide both sides of the equation by c^2, where c is the hypotenuse length. What do you obtain, in terms of trigonometric functions of x?

See the picture above.

$$\frac{a^2 + b^2}{c^2} = \frac{c^2}{c^2}$$

$$\frac{a^2}{c^2} + \frac{b^2}{c^2} = 1$$

$$\left(\frac{a}{c}\right)^2 + \left(\frac{b}{c}\right)^2 = 1$$

$$\cos^2 x + \sin^2 x = 1$$

(b) Now divide both sides of the Pythagorean Theorem by a^2, where a is one of the legs. What do you obtain, in terms of trigonometric functions of x?

$$\frac{a^2 + b^2}{a^2} = \frac{c^2}{a^2} \Rightarrow 1 + \left(\frac{b}{a}\right)^2 = \left(\frac{c}{a}\right)^2 \Rightarrow 1 + \tan^2 x = \sec^2 x.$$

(c) Deduce the third Pythagorean Identity. How did you do it?

By dividing both sides of the Pythagorean Theorem by b^2, we obtain $\cot^2 x + 1 = \csc^2 x$.

(d) One consequence of this standard is that any of these three trigonometric equations is equivalent to any other one. How can you transform $1 + \tan^2 x = \sec^2 x$ into $\sin^2 x + \cos^2 x = 1$ in one step? We can multiply both sides by $\cos^2 x$.

$$\cos^2 x (1 + \tan^2 x) = (\sec^2 x) \cos^2 x$$

$$\cos^2 x + \cos^2 x \left(\frac{\sin^2 x}{\cos^2 x}\right) = \frac{\cos^2 x}{\cos^2 x}$$

$$\cos^2 x + \sin^2 x = 1.$$

b. Prove and apply the sine, cosine, and tangent sum formulas for all real values

1. What are the sine, cosine, and tangent sum formulas?

$$\sin(x + y) = \sin x \cos y + \cos x \sin y$$

$$\cos(x + y) = \cos x \cos y - \sin x \sin y$$

$$\tan(x + y) = \frac{\tan x + \tan y}{1 - \tan x \tan y}$$

2. How are the sine, cosine, and tangent sum formulas derived?

Usually, one of the formulas is derived and then the others follow as a consequence. We will outline a proof of the formula for $\cos(A - B)$ and then use it to derive the others. (Later, we'll see how to derive these formulas from DeMoivre's Theorem.)

Suppose angle A is bigger than angle B and consider the following points on the unit circle: $(\cos A, \sin A)$, $(\cos B, \sin B)$, $(\cos(A - B), \sin(A - B))$, and $(1, 0)$.

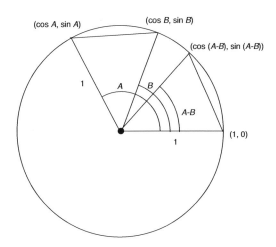

Since both chords have central angle $A - B$, the distance from $(\cos A, \sin A)$ to $(\cos B, \sin B)$ is equal to the distance from $(1, 0)$ to $(\cos(A - B), \sin(A - B))$. Setting these two distances equal (then squaring both sides) gives:

$$
\begin{aligned}
(\cos A - \cos B)^2 + (\sin A - \sin B)^2 &= (\cos(A - B) - 1)^2 + \sin^2(A - B) \\
\cos^2 A - 2\cos A \cos B + \cos^2 B + \sin^2 A & - 2\sin A \sin B + \sin^2 B = \\
&= \cos^2(A - B) - 2\cos(A - B) + 1 + \sin^2(A - B) \\
2 - 2\cos A \cos B - 2\sin A \sin B &= 2 - 2\cos(A - B),
\end{aligned}
$$

where we have repeatedly used the Pythagorean identity $\cos^2 x + \sin^2 x = 1$. It follows that

$$
\cos(A - B) = \cos A \cos B + \sin A \sin B.
$$

Now, to find $\cos(x + y)$, use the formula with $A = x$ and $B = -y$.

3. How do you apply these sum formulas?

One way is to use the cosine of a sum formula to derive the formula for the sine of a sum, and then for the tangent of a sum, etc. See the Sample Problems for problems along these lines. Another way to apply them is to derive the double-angle and half-angle formulas. These will be explained in section **g.** below.

Yet another way that these formulas can be applied is to calculate more exact values for trigonometric functions without using a calculator. For example, if we know the values of sine and cosine at $\dfrac{\pi}{3}$ and $\dfrac{\pi}{4}$, then we can find other values, like $\cos\left(\dfrac{\pi}{12}\right)$, using the difference formula we just derived above. First, notice that another way to write $\dfrac{\pi}{12}$ is as $\dfrac{\pi}{3} - \dfrac{\pi}{4}$. So,

$$
\begin{aligned}
\cos\left(\frac{\pi}{12}\right) = \cos\left(\frac{\pi}{3} - \frac{\pi}{4}\right) &= \cos\left(\frac{\pi}{3}\right)\cos\left(\frac{\pi}{4}\right) + \sin\left(\frac{\pi}{3}\right)\sin\left(\frac{\pi}{4}\right) \\
&= \left(\frac{1}{2}\right)\left(\frac{\sqrt{2}}{2}\right) + \left(\frac{\sqrt{3}}{2}\right)\left(\frac{\sqrt{2}}{2}\right) \\
&= \frac{\sqrt{2} + \sqrt{6}}{4}.
\end{aligned}
$$

4. Sample Problems

   (a) Using the identity $\sin x = \cos(\frac{\pi}{2} - x)$ and the formula for the cosine of a sum or difference, derive the formula for $\sin(x + y)$.

   (b) Derive formulas for $\sin(x - y)$, $\cos(x - y)$, and $\tan(x - y)$ from the sum formulas.

   (c) Show that $\cos(0) = 1$ and that $\sin(0) = \tan(0) = 0$. [Hint: find $\cos(x - x)$.]

   (d) We know that in general, $\sin(x + y) \neq \sin x + \sin y$. But can you find specific values of x and y that would make the equation true?

   (e) We know that in general, $\cos(x + y) \neq \cos x + \cos y$. But can you find specific values of x and y that would make the equation true?

   (f) Derive a formula for $\cot(x + y)$.

   (g) Find exact values for $\sin\left(\dfrac{\pi}{12}\right)$, $\cos\left(\dfrac{7\pi}{12}\right)$, and $\cos\left(\dfrac{5\pi}{12}\right)$.

5. Answers to Sample Problems

   (a) Using the identity $\sin x = \cos(\frac{\pi}{2} - x)$ and the formula for the cosine of a sum or difference, derive the formula for $\sin(x + y)$.

$$\begin{aligned}
\sin(x + y) &= \cos\left(\frac{\pi}{2} - (x + y)\right) = \cos\left(\left(\frac{\pi}{2} - x\right) - y\right) \\
&= \cos\left(\frac{\pi}{2} - x\right)\cos y + \sin\left(\frac{\pi}{2} - x\right)\sin y \\
&= \sin x \cos y + \cos x \sin y
\end{aligned}$$

   (b) Derive formulas for $\sin(x - y)$, $\cos(x - y)$, and $\tan(x - y)$ from the sum formulas. Notice that we use the fact that sine and tangent are odd functions, while cosine is even. See the next section for more details.

$$\sin(x - y) = \sin(x + (-y)) = \sin x \cos(-y) + \cos x \sin(-y) = \sin x \cos y - \cos x \sin y.$$

$$\cos(x - y) = \cos x \cos(-y) - \sin x \sin(-y) = \cos x \cos y + \sin x \sin y.$$

$$\tan(x - y) = \frac{\tan x + \tan(-y)}{1 - \tan x \tan(-y)} = \frac{\tan x - \tan y}{1 + \tan x \tan y}.$$

   (c) Show that $\cos(0) = 1$ and that $\sin(0) = \tan(0) = 0$. [Hint: find $\cos(x - x)$.]

$$\cos(0) = \cos(x - x) = \cos^2 x + \sin^2 x = 1.$$

$$\sin(0) = \sin(x - x) = \sin x \cos x - \cos x \sin x = 0.$$

$$\tan(0) = \tan(x - x) = \frac{\tan x - \tan x}{1 + \tan^2 x} = \frac{0}{\sec^2 x} = 0.$$

   (d) We know that in general, $\sin(x + y) \neq \sin x + \sin y$. But can you find specific values of x and y that would make the equation true? Yes, if x (or y) is equal to any multiple of 2π, then the equation is true.

(e) We know that in general, $\cos(x+y) \neq \cos x + \cos y$. But can you find specific values of x and y that would make the equation true? Yes, if $x = \frac{\pi}{3}$ and $y = -\frac{\pi}{3}$, then $x + y = 0$. So, $\cos(x+y) = 1$ and $\cos(\frac{\pi}{3}) + \cos(-\frac{\pi}{3}) = \frac{1}{2} + \frac{1}{2} = 1$. There are others.

(f) Derive a formula for $\cot(x+y)$. Answers may vary.

$$\cot(x+y) = \frac{\cos(x+y)}{\sin(x+y)} = \frac{\cos x \cos y - \sin x \sin y}{\sin x \cos y + \cos x \sin y} = \frac{\cot x \cot y - 1}{\cot x + \cot y}.$$

(g) Find exact values for $\sin\left(\frac{\pi}{12}\right)$, $\cos\left(\frac{7\pi}{12}\right)$, and $\cos\left(\frac{5\pi}{12}\right)$. Solution methods may vary, but the answers should not.

$$\begin{aligned}
\sin\left(\frac{\pi}{12}\right) = \sin\left(\frac{\pi}{3} - \frac{\pi}{4}\right) &= \sin\left(\frac{\pi}{3}\right)\cos\left(\frac{\pi}{4}\right) - \cos\left(\frac{\pi}{3}\right)\sin\left(\frac{\pi}{4}\right) \\
&= \left(\frac{\sqrt{3}}{2}\right)\left(\frac{\sqrt{2}}{2}\right) - \left(\frac{1}{2}\right)\left(\frac{\sqrt{2}}{2}\right) \\
&= \frac{\sqrt{6} - \sqrt{2}}{4}.
\end{aligned}$$

$$\begin{aligned}
\cos\left(\frac{7\pi}{12}\right) = \cos\left(\frac{\pi}{3} + \frac{\pi}{4}\right) &= \cos\left(\frac{\pi}{3}\right)\cos\left(\frac{\pi}{4}\right) - \sin\left(\frac{\pi}{3}\right)\sin\left(\frac{\pi}{4}\right) \\
&= \left(\frac{1}{2}\right)\left(\frac{\sqrt{2}}{2}\right) - \left(\frac{\sqrt{3}}{2}\right)\left(\frac{\sqrt{2}}{2}\right) \\
&= \frac{\sqrt{2} - \sqrt{6}}{4}.
\end{aligned}$$

$$\begin{aligned}
\cos\left(\frac{5\pi}{12}\right) = \cos\left(\frac{2\pi}{3} - \frac{\pi}{4}\right) &= \cos\left(\frac{2\pi}{3}\right)\cos\left(\frac{\pi}{4}\right) + \sin\left(\frac{2\pi}{3}\right)\sin\left(\frac{\pi}{4}\right) \\
&= \left(-\frac{1}{2}\right)\left(\frac{\sqrt{2}}{2}\right) + \left(\frac{\sqrt{3}}{2}\right)\left(\frac{\sqrt{2}}{2}\right) \\
&= \frac{-\sqrt{2} + \sqrt{6}}{4}.
\end{aligned}$$

c. Analyze properties of trigonometric functions in a variety of ways (e.g., graphing and solving problems, using the unit circle)

1. What are some properties of the sine and cosine functions? How do these properties show up on a graph?

   Sine and cosine functions are periodic with fundamental period 2π. That means that, for any value of x, $f(x+2\pi) = f(x)$ whenever f is a basic sine or cosine function. These functions are also bounded between -1 and 1, which means that for any value of x, $-1 \leq f(x) \leq 1$. Also, sine and cosine are defined for all real values of x; that is, each one has a domain consisting of all real numbers. Sine is odd, and $\sin(0) = 0$, whereas cosine is even and $\cos(0) = 1$.

On a graph, $y = \sin x$ and $y = \cos x$ are typical "wave" functions. They oscillate regularly between the horizontal lines $y = 1$ and $y = -1$ and extend infinitely in both the positive and negative x-directions. The graph of $y = \sin x$ is shown below.

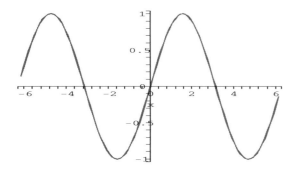

2. What are some properties of the tangent and cotangent functions? How do these properties show up on a graph?

Tangent and cotangent functions are periodic with fundamental period π. These functions are unbounded. In fact, each function has a range consisting of all real numbers. Tangent is not defined whenever cosine is zero (i.e., at $\frac{\pi}{2} + k\pi$), while cotangent is not defined whenever sine is zero (i.e., at $k\pi$), where k is any integer.

On a graph, these functions consist of several branches, each of which is a copy of the fundamental branch (between $-\frac{\pi}{2}$ and $\frac{\pi}{2}$ for tangent, between 0 and π for cotangent) that has been translated by an integer multiple of π. The branches have vertical asymptotes at the values for which they are undefined. The graph of $y = \tan x$ is shown below.

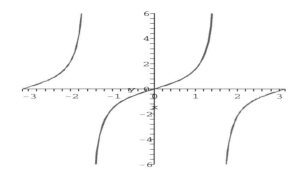

3. What are some properties of the secant and cosecant functions? How do these properties show up on a graph?

Secant and cosecant functions are periodic with fundamental period 2π. Secant (like tangent) is not defined when cosine is zero (odd multiples of $\frac{\pi}{2}$), whereas cosecant (like cotangent) is not defined when sine is zero (multiples of π). Each of the basic functions has a range of $(-\infty, -1] \cup [1, \infty)$.

On a graph, secant and cosecant have vertical asymptotes where they are not defined. They consist of disjoint U-shaped pieces, either positive and opening upward or negative and opening downward. The graph of $y = \sec x$ is shown below.

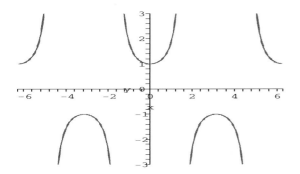

4. What are some problems that can be solved using these properties?

- $\sin x = 0$ ($x = k\pi$, where k is any integer)

- $\sin(2x) = 1$ ($2x = \dfrac{\pi}{2} + 2k\pi \Rightarrow x = \dfrac{\pi}{4} + k\pi$, where k is any integer)

- $\tan x = \sqrt{3}$ ($x = \dfrac{\pi}{3} + k\pi$, where k is any integer)

- $\sec^2 x = 2$ ($x = \dfrac{\pi}{4} + \dfrac{k\pi}{2}$, where k is any integer)

For more examples of solving trigonometry problems, see the next subsection on inverse trigonometric functions.

5. What are some problems that can be shown to be unsolvable using these properties?

- $\sin 2x = 2$ is unsolvable because the range of sine is $[-1, 1]$.

- $\cot \pi = x$ is unsolvable because cot is not defined at π ($\sin \pi = 0$)

- $\csc x = 0$ is unsolvable because $|\csc x| \geq 1$.

6. How can the unit circle be used to analyze properties of trigonometric functions?

We used the unit circle earlier to help derive the formula for the cosine of a sum. The main feature of the unit circle is that each point can either be labeled as (x, y), where $x^2 + y^2 = 1$, or as $(\cos \theta, \sin \theta)$, where θ is the central angle corresponding to the point (and measured counter-clockwise from the positive x-axis). The following diagram shows this relationship.

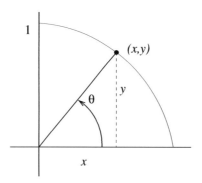

Because of the relationships $x = \cos\theta$, $y = \sin\theta$, we can use intuition about values of x and y to gain intuition about values of cosine and sine. For instance, let's pick two points that are mirror images of each other in the y-axis, and have positive y-coordinate. We know that their x-values have to have the same absolute value, but opposite signs. This corresponds to a statement about cosines. The following diagram shows the situation:

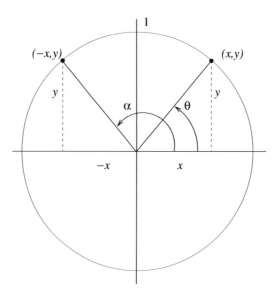

We know that $x = \cos\theta$ and $-x = \cos\alpha$ because both these points lie on the unit circle, which means that each x-coordinate is the cosine of its corresponding central angle. Substitution then tells us that $\cos\alpha = -\cos\theta$. Also, we can see from symmetry that $\theta + \alpha = \pi$ radians, or 180 degrees. If we perform an algebraic substitution of $\alpha = \pi - \theta$, then we have an identity:

$$\cos(\pi - \theta) = -\cos\theta.$$

This can also be verified using the angle difference formula for cosine, but knowing that cosines correspond to x-values on the unit circle gives us a geometric way to interpret this identity.

7. Sample Problems

   (a) Which of the six basic trigonometric functions are even (meaning $f(-x) = f(x)$)? Which are odd (meaning $f(-x) = -f(x)$)? Which are neither? [Hint: write them in terms of sine and cosine.]

(b) Solve the following equations for x. List all solutions on $[0, 2\pi]$.

    i. $\cos x = \dfrac{\sqrt{2}}{2}$

    ii. $\cos 3x = \dfrac{\sqrt{3}}{2}$

    iii. $\tan^4 x - 4\tan^2 x + 3 = 0$

    iv. $\sec x = \dfrac{1}{2}$

    v. $(\sin 2x)(\cos 2x) = \dfrac{1}{4}$

(c) List three different trig functions that have period π.

(d) List two different trig functions that have period 1 and have asymptotes at $x = n$ for any integer n.

(e) Sketch the graph of $y = -B\sin(\pi x) + B$. Label one maximum point on the graph, one minimum, and all intercepts.

(f) Using the unit circle, explain why $\sin(\pi + \theta) + \sin(\pi - \theta) = 0$.

8. Answers to Sample Problems

  (a) Which of the six basic trigonometric functions are even (meaning $f(-x) = f(x)$)? Which are odd (meaning $f(-x) = -f(x)$)? Which are neither? [Hint: write them in terms of sine and cosine.] The functions $\sin x$, $\tan x$, $\cot x$ and $\csc x$ are odd, while $\cos x$ and $\sec x$ are even.

  (b) Solve the following equations for x. List all solutions on $[0, 2\pi]$.

    i. $\cos x = \dfrac{\sqrt{2}}{2}$; $x = \dfrac{\pi}{4}, \dfrac{7\pi}{4}$

    ii. $\cos 3x = \dfrac{\sqrt{3}}{2}$; $3x = \dfrac{\pi}{6} + 2k\pi$ or $\dfrac{11\pi}{6} + 2k\pi$; $x = \dfrac{\pi}{18}, \dfrac{11\pi}{18}, \dfrac{13\pi}{18}, \dfrac{23\pi}{18}, \dfrac{25\pi}{18}, \dfrac{35\pi}{18}$

    iii. $\tan^4 x - 4\tan^2 x + 3 = 0$; $(\tan^2 x - 1)(\tan^2 x - 3) = 0$; $\tan x = \pm 1, \pm\sqrt{3}$;
    $x = \dfrac{\pi}{4}, \dfrac{\pi}{3}, \dfrac{2\pi}{3}, \dfrac{3\pi}{4}, \dfrac{5\pi}{4}, \dfrac{4\pi}{3}, \dfrac{5\pi}{3}, \dfrac{7\pi}{4}$

    iv. $\sec x = \dfrac{1}{2}$; No solutions. ($|\sec x| \geq 1$)

    v. $(\sin 2x)(\cos 2x) = \dfrac{1}{4}$; $\sin 4x = \dfrac{1}{2}$; $x = \dfrac{\pi}{24}, \dfrac{5\pi}{24}, \dfrac{13\pi}{24}, \dfrac{17\pi}{24}, \dfrac{25\pi}{24}, \dfrac{29\pi}{24}, \dfrac{37\pi}{24}, \dfrac{41\pi}{24}$

  (c) List three different trig functions that have period π. Answers include $\tan x$, $\cot x$, $\sin 2x$, $\cos 2x$, etc.

  (d) List two different trig functions that have period 1 and have asymptotes at $x = n$ for any integer n. Answers include $\cot(\pi x)$, $\tan(\pi x - \frac{\pi}{2})$, $\csc(2\pi x)$, etc.

  (e) Sketch the graph of $y = -B\sin(\pi x) + B$. Label one maximum point on the graph, one minimum, and all intercepts.

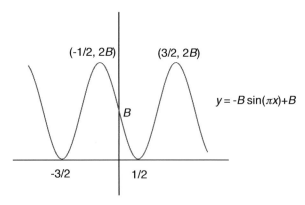

(f) Using the unit circle, explain why $\sin(\pi + \theta) + \sin(\pi - \theta) = 0$. Recall that π radians corresponds to 180 degrees, which lies on the negative x-axis. Notice that the angles $\pi + \theta$ and $\pi - \theta$ correspond to rays that are mirror images in the x-axis, and thus intersect the unit circle in two points that have the same x-coordinate but opposite y coordinates. (In the picture below, θ corresponds to an acute angle, but the property holds for any value of θ.)

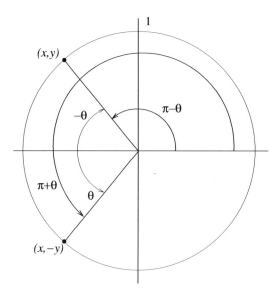

Since the two y-values have opposite signs, their sum must be zero. We know that on the unit circle, y-values correspond to values of sine. Therefore $\sin(\pi + \theta) + \sin(\pi - \theta) = 0$.

d. Apply the definitions and properties of inverse trigonometric functions (i.e., arcsin, arccos, and arctan)

1. What is the definition of an inverse trigonometric function? What are some properties of inverse trigonometric functions?

Inverse trigonometric functions are just inverse functions of trigonometric functions. For example, $\sin(\pi/4) = \sqrt{2}/2$. Therefore, $\arcsin(\sqrt{2}/2) = \pi/4$. The inverse sine (or arcsine) of x is the angle measure (usually in radians) whose sine is equal to x. Other inverse trigonometric functions are similarly defined.

$$y = \arccos x \Leftrightarrow x = \cos y, \quad y = \arctan x \Leftrightarrow x = \tan y, \; etc.$$

The general inverse trigonometric functions are technically not functions at all because they are multi-valued. For example, $\arcsin(0)$ could be 0, π, $-\pi$, 2π, 5π, etc. So, in order to guarantee that the inverse trigonometric functions are honest-to-goodness functions, we agree on one of the many correct values for the function and we call it the "principal" value (denoted as Arcsin, for instance). $\text{Arcsin}\left(-\dfrac{\sqrt{3}}{2}\right) = -\dfrac{\pi}{3}$ instead of $\dfrac{4\pi}{3}$ or $\dfrac{5\pi}{3}$, even though these satisfy $\sin\theta = -\dfrac{\sqrt{3}}{2}$.

WARNING! There are four different notations for each inverse trigonometric function. The first two are identical: $\arcsin x = \sin^{-1} x$; each one means an angle whose sine is equal to x. The principal arcsine, $\text{Arcsin}\, x = \text{Sin}^{-1} x$ is the angle between $-\dfrac{\pi}{2}$ and $\dfrac{\pi}{2}$ whose sine is x. Notice that the $\text{Arcsin}\, x$ has only one answer.

WARNING! $\sin^{-1} x \neq \dfrac{1}{\sin x}$. To say $\dfrac{1}{\sin x}$, one would write $\csc x$ or $(\sin x)^{-1}$.

The following table lists domains and ranges of the principal inverse trigonometric functions.

Function	Domain	Range
Arcsin x	$[-1, 1]$	$\left[-\dfrac{\pi}{2}, \dfrac{\pi}{2}\right]$
Arccos x	$[-1, 1]$	$[0, \pi]$
Arctan x	all reals	$\left(-\dfrac{\pi}{2}, \dfrac{\pi}{2}\right)$
Arccot x	all reals	$(0, \pi)$
Arcsec x	$(-\infty, -1] \cup [1, \infty)$	$\left[0, \dfrac{\pi}{2}\right) \cup \left(\dfrac{\pi}{2}, \pi\right]$
Arccsc x	$(-\infty, -1] \cup [1, \infty)$	$\left[-\dfrac{\pi}{2}, 0\right) \cup \left(0, \dfrac{\pi}{2}\right]$

2. How can you apply the definitions and properties to solve problems?

As an example, we'll find all the solutions to $\sin(5x) = 0.5$ with $0 \le x \le 2\pi$. First, we have $5x = \text{Arcsin}(0.5) + 2k\pi = \dfrac{\pi}{6} + 2k\pi$. Solving for x gives $x = \dfrac{\pi}{30} + \dfrac{2k\pi}{5}$. Notice that if $k = 0, 1, 2, 3, 4$, then the value of x still lies between 0 and 2π. So we get five answers, one for each value of x. Namely, x is in the set $\left\{\dfrac{\pi}{30}, \dfrac{13\pi}{30}, \dfrac{5\pi}{6}, \dfrac{37\pi}{30}, \dfrac{49\pi}{30}\right\}$.

But is that all the answers possible? Actually, if we look at the sine graph, there are TWO possible values for $\arcsin(0.5)$, $\dfrac{\pi}{6}$ and $\dfrac{5\pi}{6}$. So we could get $5x = \dfrac{5\pi}{6} + 2k\pi$. Again, notice that we get five values for x, corresponding to $k = 0, 1, 2, 3, 4$. This gives us five more solutions: $\dfrac{\pi}{6}, \dfrac{17\pi}{30}, \dfrac{29\pi}{30}, \dfrac{41\pi}{30}, \dfrac{53\pi}{30}$.

So, there are ten solutions to $\sin(5x) = 0.5$ between 0 and 2π. The solution set is

$$\left\{\dfrac{\pi}{30}, \dfrac{\pi}{6}, \dfrac{13\pi}{30}, \dfrac{17\pi}{30}, \dfrac{5\pi}{6}, \dfrac{29\pi}{30}, \dfrac{37\pi}{30}, \dfrac{41\pi}{30}, \dfrac{49\pi}{30}, \dfrac{53\pi}{30}\right\}.$$

3. Sample Problems

    (a) Sketch graphs of $y = \arcsin x$, $y = \arccos x$, and $y = \arctan x$.

    (b) Sketch graphs of $y = \text{Arcsin}\, x$, $y = \text{Arccos}\, x$, and $y = \text{Arctan}\, x$, and compare to the previous graphs.

    (c) Simplify, if possible.

        i. $\text{Arcsin}(-\frac{1}{2})$

        ii. $\text{Arctan}(1)$

        iii. $\text{Arctan}(\sqrt{3}) + \text{Arccos}(-1)$

        iv. $\text{Arcsin}(2)$

        v. $\cos(\pi - \text{Arccos}(-\frac{\sqrt{3}}{2}))$

        vi. $\text{Arcsin}(\cos(\frac{5\pi}{6}))$

        vii. $\text{Arcsec}(-1) - \text{Arctan}(\tan(\pi))$

    (d) True or False? If true, explain why. If false, give a counterexample. Remember, in math, "true" means "always true."

        i. $\sin(\text{Arcsin}\, x) = x$.

        ii. $\text{Arctan}(\tan x) = x$.

        iii. $\text{Arctan}(\frac{\pi}{2})$ is undefined.

        iv. $\arctan x = 1$ has two solutions between 0 and 2π.

        v. $\text{Arctan}\, {-3} = x$ has two solutions between 0 and 2π.

        vi. If $x \neq 0$, then $\tan(\text{Arccos}\, x) = \dfrac{\sqrt{1-x^2}}{x}$.

        vii. The value of $\sin x$ is never negative on the range of $\text{Arccos}\, x$.

4. Answers to Sample Problems

    (a) Sketch graphs of $y = \arcsin x$, $y = \arccos x$, and $y = \arctan x$.

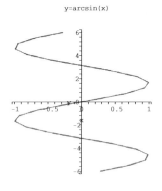 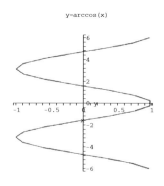 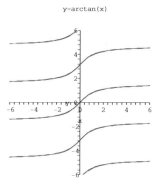

    (b) Sketch graphs of $y = \text{Arcsin}\, x$, $y = \text{Arccos}\, x$, and $y = \text{Arctan}\, x$, and compare to the previous graphs.

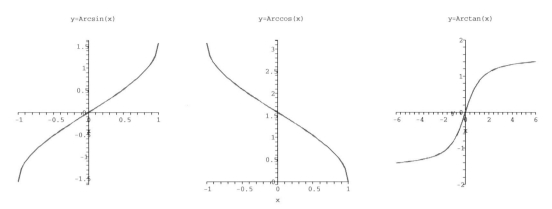

The difference is that the principal arc-graphs are single-valued. For every value of x, there is only one value of y. This makes the principal inverse trigonometric functions into actual functions. The other graphs are merely relations.

(c) Simplify, if possible.

i. $\text{Arcsin}(-\frac{1}{2}) = -\frac{\pi}{6}$

ii. $\text{Arctan}(1) = \frac{\pi}{4}$

iii. $\text{Arctan}(\sqrt{3}) + \text{Arccos}(-1) = \frac{\pi}{3} + \pi = \frac{4\pi}{3}$

iv. $\text{Arcsin}(2)$ is not defined because $\sin x$ cannot equal 2.

v. $\cos(\pi - \text{Arccos}(-\frac{\sqrt{3}}{2})) = \cos(\pi - \frac{5\pi}{6}) = \frac{\sqrt{3}}{2}$

vi. $\text{Arcsin}(\cos(\frac{5\pi}{6})) = -\frac{\pi}{3}$

vii. $\text{Arcsec}(-1) - \text{Arctan}(\tan(\pi)) = \pi - 0 = \pi$

(d) True or False? If true, explain why. If false, give a counterexample. Remember, in math, "true" means "always true."

i. $\sin(\text{Arcsin } x) = x$. TRUE. $\text{Arcsin } x$ is an angle whose sine is x.

ii. $\text{Arctan}(\tan x) = x$. FALSE. $\text{Arctan}(\tan \pi) = \text{Arctan}(0) = 0 \neq \pi$.

iii. $\text{Arctan}(\frac{\pi}{2})$ is undefined. FALSE. The tangent of $\frac{\pi}{2}$ is undefined. $\text{Arctan}(\frac{\pi}{2})$ is close to 1 because $\tan(1) \approx \frac{\pi}{2}$.

iv. $\arctan x = 1$ has two solutions between 0 and 2π. FALSE. If $\arctan x = 1$, then $\tan 1 = x$. Since tangent is a function, there is only one value for x.

v. $\text{Arctan} -3 = x$ has two solutions between 0 and 2π. FALSE. $\text{Arctan} -3$ is uniquely defined via the principal arctangent function.

vi. If $x \neq 0$, then $\tan(\text{Arccos } x) = \dfrac{\sqrt{1-x^2}}{x}$. TRUE. If $y = \text{Arccos } x$, then $\cos y = x$ and $0 \leq y \leq \pi$. So, $\sin y = \sqrt{1 - \cos^2 y} = \sqrt{1 - x^2}$. Hence $\tan y = \frac{\sqrt{1-x^2}}{x}$.

vii. The value of $\sin x$ is never negative on the range of $\text{Arccos } x$. TRUE. The range of $\text{Arccos } x$ is $[0, \pi]$, on which sine is positive. Similarly, cosine is never negative on the range of $\text{Arcsin } x$.

e. Apply polar representations of complex numbers (e.g., DeMoivre's Theorem)

1. What are polar coordinates?

   Polar coordinates are another way to describe points on the plane (rather than using Cartesian (x, y) coordinates). A point is described by the ordered pair (r, θ), where r describes how far the point is from the origin, and θ describes the angle formed by the ray leading from the origin to the point and the ray of the positive x-axis (measured counter-clockwise starting at the positive x-axis). As examples, the Cartesian point $(0, -2)$ corresponds to the polar point $(2, \frac{3\pi}{2})$ (or possibly $(2, -\frac{\pi}{2})$), and the Cartesian point $(3, 3)$ corresponds to the polar point $(3\sqrt{2}, \frac{\pi}{4})$.

   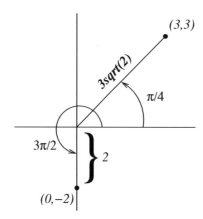

   The formulas for writing x and y as functions of r and θ are therefore...

   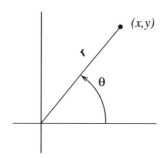

   - $x =$

   - $y =$

   ANS: $x = r \cos \theta$, $y = r \sin \theta$.

2. How do you connect trigonometry to complex numbers?

   Often, complex numbers (e.g., $2 - 3i$) can be graphed as points on a Cartesian plane (e.g., $(2, -3)$). The $a + bi$ notation is helpful when adding or subtracting complex numbers. (Recall that $i^2 = -1$.) But the polar coordinates are often more helpful when multiplying, dividing, or finding roots of complex numbers. Using the two examples listed above, we can write complex numbers in terms of r and θ. First we factor out $r = \sqrt{a^2 + b^2}$ and then we write the other factor in terms of trigonometric functions of θ.

- $(0, -2) \to -2\mathbf{i} = 2(0 + \mathbf{i}(-1)) = 2(\cos(\frac{3\pi}{2}) + \mathbf{i}\sin(\frac{3\pi}{2}))$
- $(3, 3) \to 3 + 3\mathbf{i} = 3\sqrt{2}(\frac{\sqrt{2}}{2} + \mathbf{i}\frac{\sqrt{2}}{2}) = 3\sqrt{2}(\cos(\frac{\pi}{4}) + \mathbf{i}\sin(\frac{\pi}{4}))$

3. What is DeMoivre's Theorem? How can we use it?

   DeMoivre's Theorem: If x is a real number, and if n is an integer, then

   $$(\cos x + \mathbf{i}\sin x)^n = \cos(nx) + \mathbf{i}\sin(nx),$$

   where $\mathbf{i}^2 = -1$. If $(\cos x + \mathbf{i}\sin x)$ is abbreviated cis x, then the theorem says $(\text{cis } x)^n = \text{cis}(nx)$.

   One way to use this theorem is to derive the multiple angle formulas using complex multiplication. (See Sample Problems, below.) Another way to use the theorem is to find roots of complex numbers. For example, to find the three solutions to the equation $z^3 = 8$, we first think of z as a complex number. Then, using polar coordinates, we can write $z = r\cos\theta + \mathbf{i}r\sin\theta = r\,\text{cis}(\theta)$ Then

   $$8 = z^3 = r^3(\text{cis }\theta)^3 = r^3\,\text{cis}(3\theta).$$

   By comparing real and imaginary parts, we see that r must be a real cube root of 8, i.e. $r = 2$, and $\cos(3\theta) = 1$. [We also need $\sin(3\theta) = 0$, but this is redundant if $\cos(3\theta) = 1$.] So, $3\theta = 0, 2\pi, 4\pi$, which means $\theta = 0, \frac{2\pi}{3}, \frac{4\pi}{3}$. Therefore, the three cube roots of 8 are:

   - $2\,\text{cis}(0) = 2(1 + 0\mathbf{i}) = 2$
   - $2\,\text{cis}\left(\dfrac{2\pi}{3}\right) = 2\left(-\dfrac{1}{2} + \mathbf{i}\dfrac{\sqrt{3}}{2}\right) = -1 + \mathbf{i}\sqrt{3}$
   - $2\,\text{cis}\left(\dfrac{4\pi}{3}\right) = 2\left(-\dfrac{1}{2} - \mathbf{i}\dfrac{\sqrt{3}}{2}\right) = -1 - \mathbf{i}\sqrt{3}$

4. Sample Problems

   (a) Multiply $-2\mathbf{i}$ and $3 + 3\mathbf{i}$ using polar coordinates. Use the fact that cis x cis $y = \text{cis}(x+y)$.

   (b) Find formulas for the polar coordinates r and θ in terms of x and y.

   (c) Explain why the expression $\cos\theta + \mathbf{i}\sin\theta$ comes up when converting from Cartesian to polar representations of complex numbers.

   (d) Derive formulas for $\cos(2x)$ and $\sin(2x)$ using DeMoivre's Theorem. That is, we know $\text{cis}(2x) = (\text{cis } x)^2 = (\cos x + \mathbf{i}\sin x)^2 = \ldots$. Multiply out and simplify. Then equate the real parts and the imaginary parts of your answer with the real parts and imaginary parts of $\text{cis}(2x)$.

   (e) Find all the fourth roots of -1.

   (f) Find all the sixth roots of 64.

   (g) Find all square roots of $\mathbf{i}$.

   (h) Find all cube roots of $\mathbf{i}$.

(i) Explain how you know that you will be able to explicitly write down all complex n-th roots of positive real numbers (i.e., all solutions to $x^n = a > 0$) whenever n is 1, 2, 3, 4, 6, 8, or 12.

(j) Derive formulas for $\cos(3x)$ and $\sin(3x)$ using DeMoivre's Theorem. How far can you go?

(k) A generalization of DeMoivre's Theorem can be found in Euler's Formula: $e^{ix} = \operatorname{cis} x$. Show that $\operatorname{cis} x \operatorname{cis} y = \operatorname{cis}(x + y)$ and then use your answer to verify the formulas for $\cos(x + y)$ and $\sin(x + y)$.

5. Answers to Sample Problems

(a) Multiply $-2i$ and $3 + 3i$ using polar coordinates. Use the fact that $\operatorname{cis} x \operatorname{cis} y = \operatorname{cis}(x+y)$. First, we write the numbers in polar form: $-2i = 2 \operatorname{cis} \frac{3\pi}{2}$ and $3 + 3i = 3\sqrt{2} \operatorname{cis} \frac{\pi}{4}$. Then we multiply magnitudes and add angles, giving:

$$
\begin{aligned}
(-2i)(3 + 3i) &= \left(2 \operatorname{cis} \frac{3\pi}{2}\right)\left(3\sqrt{2} \operatorname{cis} \frac{\pi}{4}\right) = 6\sqrt{2} \operatorname{cis} \frac{7\pi}{4} \\
&= 6\sqrt{2}\left(\frac{\sqrt{2}}{2} - i\frac{\sqrt{2}}{2}\right) = 6 - 6i.
\end{aligned}
$$

(b) Find formulas for the polar coordinates r and θ in terms of x and y.

$$
r = \sqrt{x^2 + y^2}; \quad \theta = \arctan\left(\frac{y}{x}\right)
$$

(c) Explain why the expression $\cos\theta + i\sin\theta$ comes up when converting from Cartesian to polar representations of complex numbers. This expression occurs because complex numbers are graphed on a Cartesian plane in $x + iy$ form, which in polar coordinates becomes $r\cos\theta + ir\sin\theta = r(\cos\theta + i\sin\theta)$.

(d) Derive formulas for $\cos(2x)$ and $\sin(2x)$ using DeMoivre's Theorem. That is, we know $\operatorname{cis}(2x) = (\operatorname{cis} x)^2 = (\cos x + i\sin x)^2 = \ldots$. Multiply out and simplify. Then equate the real parts and the imaginary parts of your answer with the real parts and imaginary parts of $\operatorname{cis}(2x)$.

$$
\begin{aligned}
\operatorname{cis}(2x) &= (\operatorname{cis} x)^2 = (\cos x + i\sin x)^2 \\
&= \cos^2 x + 2i\sin x \cos x + i^2 \sin^2 x \\
&= (\cos^2 x - \sin^2 x) + i(2\sin x \cos x), \\
\text{but by definition, } \operatorname{cis}(2x) &= \cos 2x + i\sin 2x,
\end{aligned}
$$

which means that $\cos 2x = \cos^2 x - \sin^2 x$ and $\sin 2x = 2\sin x \cos x$.

(e) Find all the fourth roots of -1. We must solve $z^4 = -1$. Note that $-1 = \operatorname{cis}\pi$. Let $z = r \operatorname{cis}\theta$. Then $z^4 = r^4 \operatorname{cis} 4\theta$. Hence $\operatorname{cis}\pi = r^4 \operatorname{cis} 4\theta$, which means $r^4 = 1$ and $4\theta = \pi + 2k\pi$. So, $r = 1$ and $\theta = \frac{\pi}{4}, \frac{3\pi}{4}, \frac{5\pi}{4}, \frac{7\pi}{4}$. Hence $z = \pm\frac{\sqrt{2}}{2} \pm i\frac{\sqrt{2}}{2}$ (where all sign combinations are possible).

(f) Find all the sixth roots of 64. We must solve $z^6 = 64$. Again, note that $64 = 64\operatorname{cis}(0)$. Let $z = r\operatorname{cis}\theta$. Then $z^6 = r^6\operatorname{cis}6\theta$. Hence $64\operatorname{cis}0 = r^6\operatorname{cis}6\theta$. Thus $r^6 = 64$ and $6\theta = 0 + 2k\pi$. So, $r = 2$ and $\theta = 0, \frac{\pi}{3}, \frac{2\pi}{3}, \pi, \frac{4\pi}{3}, \frac{5\pi}{3}$. Therefore, $z = \pm 2$ or $\pm 1 \pm i\sqrt{3}$ (again, with all possible sign combinations).

(g) Find all square roots of $\mathbf{i}$. We must solve $z^2 = \mathbf{i}$. Note that $\mathbf{i} = \operatorname{cis}(\frac{\pi}{2})$. Following the same method as above, we obtain $r^2 = 1$ and $2\theta = \frac{\pi}{2} + 2k\pi$. So $r = 1$ and $\theta = \frac{\pi}{4}$ or $\frac{5\pi}{4}$, which means that the square roots of $\mathbf{i}$ are $\pm(\frac{\sqrt{2}}{2} + \mathbf{i}\frac{\sqrt{2}}{2})$.

(h) Find all cube roots of $\mathbf{i}$. We must solve $z^3 = \mathbf{i}$. Starting similarly to the previous problem, we find that $r = 1$ and $3\theta = \frac{\pi}{2} + 2k\pi$, which means $\theta = \frac{\pi}{6}, \frac{5\pi}{6}, \frac{3\pi}{2}$. Therefore, the cube roots of $\mathbf{i}$ are $\frac{\sqrt{3}}{2} + \mathbf{i}(\frac{1}{2})$, $-\frac{\sqrt{3}}{2} + \mathbf{i}(\frac{1}{2})$ and $-\mathbf{i}$.

(i) Explain how you know that you will be able to explicitly write down all complex n-th roots of positive real numbers (i.e., all solutions to $x^n = a > 0$) whenever n is 1, 2, 3, 4, 6, 8, or 12.

We know that we will be able to write down all n-th roots of a positive real number whenever $\theta = \frac{2\pi}{n}$ is one of the "nice" angles for which sine and cosine have known values, that is for any multiples of $\frac{\pi}{4}$ or $\frac{\pi}{6}$. This means that n is any factor of 8 or 12.

(j) Derive formulas for $\cos(3x)$ and $\sin(3x)$ using DeMoivre's Theorem. How far can you go? We could go as far as we want, so long as we can multiply out the resulting binomial. For this problem, we want to compare $\operatorname{cis}3x$, that is, $\cos 3x + \mathbf{i}\sin 3x$, with the equal expression $(\operatorname{cis}x)^3 = (\cos x + \mathbf{i}\sin x)^3$.

$$
\begin{aligned}
(\cos x + \mathbf{i}\sin x)^3 &= \cos^3 x + 3\mathbf{i}\cos^2 x \sin x + 3\mathbf{i}^2 \cos x \sin^2 x + \mathbf{i}^3 \sin^3 x \\
&= \cos^3 x + 3\mathbf{i}\cos^2 x \sin x - 3\cos x \sin^2 x - \mathbf{i}\sin^3 x \\
&= \cos^3 x - 3\cos x \sin^2 x + \mathbf{i}(3\cos^2 x \sin x - \sin^3 x),
\end{aligned}
$$

which means $\cos 3x = \cos^3 x - 3\cos x \sin^2 x$ and $\sin 3x = 3\cos^2 x \sin x - \sin^3 x$. There are other forms of these expressions, based on $\sin^2 x + \cos^2 x = 1$.

(k) A generalization of DeMoivre's Theorem can be found in Euler's Formula: $e^{\mathbf{i}x} = \operatorname{cis}x$. Show that $\operatorname{cis}x\operatorname{cis}y = \operatorname{cis}(x+y)$ and then use your answer to verify the formulas for $\cos(x+y)$ and $\sin(x+y)$.

$$
\cos(x+y) + \mathbf{i}\sin(x+y) = \operatorname{cis}(x+y) = e^{\mathbf{i}(x+y)} = e^{\mathbf{i}x}e^{\mathbf{i}y} = \operatorname{cis}x\operatorname{cis}y.
$$

Also, we know that

$$
\begin{aligned}
\operatorname{cis}x\operatorname{cis}y &= (\cos x + \mathbf{i}\sin x)(\cos y + \mathbf{i}\sin y) \\
&= \cos x \cos y + \mathbf{i}\cos x \sin y + \mathbf{i}\sin x \cos y + \mathbf{i}^2 \sin x \sin y \\
&= (\cos x \cos y - \sin x \sin y) + \mathbf{i}(\cos x \sin y + \sin x \cos y),
\end{aligned}
$$

which means that $\cos(x+y)$ must be the real part, which equals $\cos x \cos y - \sin x \sin y$. Similarly, $\sin(x+y)$ must be the imaginary part, which equals $\cos x \sin y + \sin x \cos y$. These are precisely the angle sum formulas for cosine and sine.

f. Model periodic phenomena with periodic functions

1. What is the formula for a typical sinusoidal function?

   One form of the typical sinusoidal function is

   $$f(x) = A\cos(B(x - C)) + D,$$

   where A is the amplitude, D is the midline (or average value), C is the horizontal shift, and the period is $\frac{2\pi}{B}$. The maximum value of f is _____ and the minimum value of f is _____ .

   ANS: maximum value is $D + A$, minimum value is $D - A$

2. What situations call for a sinusoidal model?

   Sinusoidal functions oscillate regularly and symmetrically (and cyclically) around a middle value, between two extremes. For instance, the time of the sunrise in New York City as a function of the day of the year can be modeled with a sinusoidal function having a period of one year. The horizontal displacement of a pendulum also follows a sinusoidal pattern. And, if you have the kind of clock where the hands move smoothly, then the x-coordinate (or y-coordinate) of any of the clock's hands follows a sinusoidal pattern. See the Sample Problems for more examples.

3. What other periodic functions do not call for a sinusoidal model?

   If the periodic behavior does not oscillate back and forth regularly, then perhaps a trigonometric function other than sine or cosine will be needed. For instance, consider the situation where a rotating sprinkler head shoots water onto a wall a short distance away. As the sprinkler head rotates, the water jet travels across the wall. The point where the water jet hits the wall moves as a function of time, and repeats after each cycle, but it does not oscillate back and forth. See the Sample Problems for a similar situation.

4. Sample Problems

   (a) Find a model for the horizontal position (in cm) of the tip of the second hand of a stopwatch. Assume that the second hand is 2cm long, that the stopwatch is centered at the origin, and that time $t = 0$ corresponds to starting the stopwatch (i.e. with the second hand pointing upward).

   (b) Johnny observed a population of rabbits for one year. He counted a minimum of 1500 rabbits at the beginning of February and a maximum of 2700 rabbits at the beginning of August. Since he was looking for a population model, he decided on

   $$P(t) = 2700\cos\left(\frac{t - 2}{12}\right) + 1500,$$

   where t is in months and $t = 0$ corresponds to January. Correct all of Johnny's mistakes. Identify each mistake by name and provide the correct value in each instance.

   (c) A lighthouse sends out light hitting a wall that is 50 feet away from the lighthouse at its closest point. Call this closest point P. Find a formula that describes how far the light beam is horizontally from P as a function of the angle between the lighthouse and the perpendicular drawn to the wall at P.

5. Answers to Sample Problems

  (a) Find a model for x, the horizontal position (in cm) of the tip of the second hand of a stopwatch, as a function of time. Assume that the second hand is 2cm long, that the stopwatch is centered at the origin, and that time $t = 0$ corresponds to starting the stopwatch (i.e. with the second hand pointing upward). $x = 2\sin(2\pi t/60)$

There are a number of ways to approach this problem. We will follow one method here. Let's start by listing the values of x at 15-second intervals. Since the clock is centered at the origin, we know that the starting x-value is zero.

t, in sec	0	15	30	45	60
x, in cm	0	2	0	-2	0

Note that after 30 seconds, the second hand is pointing downward and so there is no horizontal displacement from where it started. (We are ignoring the y-coordinate here.) Looking at this table allows us to identify that the amplitude of x is 2cm and that the period of the motion is 60 seconds. (After 60 seconds, the values for x will start to repeat.)

If you imagine plotting these points on a graph, with the t-axis horizontal and the x-axis vertical, then you should see a sine curve emerging. So, this equation can be modeled with a sine function directly, namely $x = 2\sin(2\pi t/60)$. You could also use a cosine function that has a horizontal translation to it, or even a phase shift, if you wish. These options would give

$$x = 2\cos\left(\frac{2\pi(t-15)}{60}\right) \quad \text{or} \quad x = 2\cos\left(\frac{2\pi t}{60} - \frac{\pi}{2}\right).$$

  (b) Johnny observed a population of rabbits for one year. He counted a minimum of 1500 rabbits at the beginning of February and a maximum of 2700 rabbits at the beginning of August. Since he was looking for a population model, he decided on

$$P(t) = 2700\cos\left(\frac{t-2}{12}\right) + 1500,$$

where t is in months and $t = 0$ corresponds to January. Correct all of Johnny's mistakes. Identify each mistake by name and provide the correct value in each instance.

     i. Johnny has an incorrect amplitude of 2700. It should be 600.

    ii. Johnny has an incorrect midline of 1500. It should be 2100.

   iii. Johnny has an incorrect period of 24π. It should be 12.

   iv. Johnny has an incorrect horizontal shift. It should be 1.

    v. Johnny should be using a negative cosine graph with a horizontal shift of 1, so that he is starting at a population minimum.

   vi. The correct formula should be $P(t) = -600\cos(\frac{2\pi}{12}(t-1)) + 2100$.

(c) A lighthouse sends out light hitting a wall that is 50 feet away from the lighthouse at its closest point. Call this closest point P. Find a formula that describes how far the light beam is horizontally from P as a function of the angle between the lighthouse and the perpendicular drawn to the wall at P. $d = 50 \tan \theta$.

This time we will start by drawing a bird's-eye view of the situation.

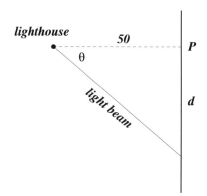

Let the angle θ be the angle between the lighthouse beam and the perpendicular to the wall. We can see a right triangle involving θ and the sides d and 50. The ratio for tangent (opposite leg divided by adjacent leg) relates all of these quantities. So we have $\tan \theta = \dfrac{d}{50}$, or $d = 50 \tan \theta$.

g. Recognize equivalent identities, including applications of the half-angle and double-angle formulas for sines and cosines

1. What does it mean for identities to be equivalent?

   Two identities are equivalent if one of them can be transformed into the other using valid algebraic and trigonometric identities and properties.

2. How do you recognize equivalent identities?

   One would have to identify the steps that take one identity to another in order to see their equivalence. We have already seen this in part **a.** above, which lists three equivalent versions of the Pythagorean trigonometric identity $\sin^2 \theta + \cos^2 \theta = 1$. These equivalent identities are obtained by dividing each side of the equation by the same function. Another example will be seen below, in the formulas for $\cos 2x$.

3. How are the double angle formulas deduced?

   Each of the double angle formulas is deduced by calculating $\sin(x + x)$, $\cos(x + x)$, and $\tan(x + x)$ using the sum formulas given above in part **b.**

   - $\sin 2x = \sin(x + x) = \sin x \cos x + \cos x \sin x = 2 \sin x \cos x$
   - $\cos 2x = \cos x \cos x - \sin x \sin x = \cos^2 x - \sin^2 x = 2 \cos^2 x - 1 = 1 - 2 \sin^2 x$
   - $\tan 2x = \frac{\sin(2x)}{\cos(2x)} = \frac{2 \sin x \cos x}{\cos^2 x - \sin^2 x} \left[\frac{\sec^2 x}{\sec^2 x} \right] = \frac{2 \tan x}{1 - \tan^2 x}$, where the answer is in terms of $\tan x$

4. Why are there three formulas for $\cos 2x$?

   This is a great example of equivalent identities. You can transform one formula for $\cos 2x$ into another by applying the identity $\sin^2 \theta + \cos^2 \theta = 1$. In particular, if you use substitution of $1 - \cos^2 x$ for $\sin^2 x$ or $1 - \sin^2 x$ for $\cos^2 x$, then you will be able to obtain all the equivalent identities.

5. How are the half angle formulas deduced?

   The half angle formulas stem from the three forms of the $\cos(2x)$ identity. For example, to obtain the formula for $\sin(x/2)$, we start with $\cos(2\theta) = 1 - 2\sin^2 \theta$ and then we solve the equation for $\sin \theta$.

   $$\cos(2\theta) = 1 - 2\sin^2 \theta \Rightarrow 2\sin^2 \theta = 1 - \cos(2\theta) \Rightarrow \sin^2 \theta = \frac{1 - \cos(2\theta)}{2}$$

   $$\sin \theta = \pm\sqrt{\frac{1 - \cos(2\theta)}{2}}$$

   Now, if we let $\theta = \frac{x}{2}$, then we obtain $\sin(x/2) = \pm\sqrt{\frac{1 - \cos x}{2}}$. The specific choice of sign ($+$ or $-$) depends on the quadrant in which $\frac{x}{2}$ lies.

   The $\cos(x/2)$ formula is derived similarly. Try to find it below.

   $$\cos(2\theta) = 2\cos^2 \theta - 1 \Rightarrow \ldots$$

   $$\cos(x/2) =$$

   ANS: $\cos(x/2) = \pm\sqrt{\frac{1+\cos x}{2}}$. Again, the choice of sign depends on the quadrant in which $\frac{x}{2}$ lies.

   Dividing these two leads to a half-angle formula for tangent. Try to find it below.

   $$\tan(x/2) =$$

   ANS: $\tan(x/2) = \pm\sqrt{\frac{1-\cos x}{1+\cos x}}$. Again, the choice of sign depends on the quadrant in which $\frac{x}{2}$ lies.

6. Sample Problems

   (a) Write down several different expressions, each of which is equal to $\cos(4x)$.

   (b) Write down three different expressions, each of which is equal to $\sin^2(2x)$.

   (c) Derive a formula for $\csc(2x)$.

   (d) Are the following identities equivalent? Explain.

   $$\sin^2 \theta + \cos^2 \theta = 1 \quad \text{and} \quad \tan^2 \theta = (\sec \theta + 1)(\sec \theta - 1)$$

7. Answers to Sample Problems

(a) Write down several different expressions, each of which is equal to $\cos(4x)$. Answers include: $\cos^2(2x) - \sin^2(2x)$, $2\cos^2(2x) - 1$, $1 - 2\sin^2(2x)$, $2(2\cos^2 x - 1)^2 - 1 = 8\cos^4 x - 8\cos^2 x + 1$. There are more.

(b) Write down three different expressions, each of which is equal to $\sin^2(2x)$. Answers include: $4\sin^2 x \cos^2 x$, $1 - \cos^2(2x)$, $4(1 - \cos^2 x)\cos^2 x = 4\cos^2 x - 4\cos^4 x$, $4\sin^2 x - 4\sin^4 x$, etc.

(c) Derive a formula for $\csc(2x)$. Answers may vary.

$$\csc 2x = \frac{1}{\sin 2x} = \frac{1}{2\sin x \cos x} = \frac{1}{2}\csc x \sec x.$$

(d) Are the following identities equivalent? Explain.

$$\sin^2\theta + \cos^2\theta = 1 \quad \text{and} \quad \tan^2\theta = (\sec\theta + 1)(\sec\theta - 1)$$

Yes, these are equivalent provided that $\cos\theta \neq 0$. (Otherwise $\tan\theta$ and $\sec\theta$ would be undefined.) Let us start with the second identity and transform it using algebra and trigonometry.

$$
\begin{aligned}
\tan^2\theta &= (\sec\theta + 1)(\sec\theta - 1) \\
\tan^2\theta &= \sec^2\theta - 1 \\
1 + \tan^2\theta &= \sec^2\theta \\
\frac{\cos^2\theta}{\cos^2\theta} + \frac{\sin^2\theta}{\cos^2\theta} &= \frac{1}{\cos^2\theta} \\
\frac{\cos^2\theta + \sin^2\theta}{\cos^2\theta} &= \frac{1}{\cos^2\theta}
\end{aligned}
$$

This last equation can be multiplied by $\cos^2\theta$ to obtain the Pythagorean identity.

5.2 Limits and Continuity

a. Derive basic properties of limits and continuity, including the Sum, Difference, Product, Constant Multiple, and Quotient Rules, using the formal definition of a limit

1. What is the formal definition of a limit?

   The notion of a limit provides one way to describe precisely the behavior of functions near asymptotes or as the variable value increases without bound. It is a way of talking about the infinite without using infinity. We say $\lim_{x \to c} f(x) = L$ if and only if, for any $\epsilon > 0$, there exists a $\delta > 0$ satisfying: if $0 < |x - c| < \delta$ then $|f(x) - L| < \epsilon$. Informally, we write $f(x) \to L$ as $x \to c$.

   This means that no matter how close you want the values of $f(x)$ to get to L, you can always find a small enough interval around $x = c$ so that every function value for x in that interval (except maybe at c) lies within your desired closeness to L.

   An example: $\lim_{x \to 2} 2x = 4$. Here's why. Say you want to find a small interval on the x-axis, centered at 2, on which $2x$ is within 0.1 of 4. Can you do it? Yes. You can pick $\delta = 0.05$. Can you always find such an interval, regardless of how accurate your estimate needs to be? (Yes, if you pick $\delta = \frac{\epsilon}{2}$.) So the limit is equal to 4.

2. How are limits related to continuity of functions? How do discontinuities relate to limits?

   While the practical idea of continuity relates to the real world ("You can draw the graph without lifting your pencil."), the mathematical definition of continuity depends on limits. We say that $f(x)$ is continuous at $x = c$ if $\lim_{x \to c} f(x) = f(c)$.

   From the fact that $\lim_{x \to 2} 2x = 4 = 2(2)$, you can determine that $2x$ is continuous at $x = 2$. You can also see that $\frac{1}{x}$ must be discontinuous at $x = 0$, because $f(0) = \frac{1}{0}$ is not defined.

3. What are the basic properties of limits and continuity?

   The basic properties are that, when each individual limit is defined, then you can perform arithmetic on them. Limits can be added, subtracted, multiplied, divided, and raised to powers (provided these operations are defined). Suppose that $\lim_{x \to c} f(x) = F$ and $\lim_{x \to c} g(x) = G$.

$$
\begin{aligned}
\lim_{x \to c}(f(x) + g(x)) &= \lim_{x \to c} f(x) + \lim_{x \to c} g(x) = F + G \\
\lim_{x \to c}(f(x) - g(x)) &= F - G \\
\lim_{x \to c}(f(x)g(x)) &= FG \\
\lim_{x \to c} \frac{f(x)}{g(x)} &= \frac{F}{G}, \quad \text{if } G \neq 0 \\
\lim_{x \to c}(kf(x)) &= kF \\
\lim_{x \to c}(f(x))^m &= F^m, \quad \text{if } F > 0
\end{aligned}
$$

When applied to continuous functions, the properties of limits become properties of continuous functions. Namely: the sum, difference, or product of continuous functions is continuous; the quotient of continuous functions is continuous, except where the denominator is zero; a constant multiple of a continuous function is continuous; and any power or root of a positive continuous function is continuous.

4. How are these properties derived from the definitions?

We'll look at the first one: $\lim_{x \to c}(f(x) + g(x)) = F + G$. [The others are similar.] Let $\epsilon > 0$. Then $\epsilon/2 > 0$. So, there exists $\delta_f > 0$ such that, if $0 < |x - c| < \delta_f$, then $|f(x) - F| < \epsilon/2$. There also exists $\delta_g > 0$ with similar properties for g. Pick δ to be the smaller of δ_f and δ_g. Suppose that $0 < |x - c| < \delta$. Then

$$|(f(x) + g(x)) - (F + G)| = |(f(x) - F) + (g(x) - G)| \le |f(x) - F| + |g(x) - G| < \frac{\epsilon}{2} + \frac{\epsilon}{2} = \epsilon.$$

So, $\lim_{x \to c}(f(x) + g(x)) = F + G$. □

Notice that we used a form of the Triangle Inequality: $|A + B| \le |A| + |B|$.

5. Sample Problems

(a) Find the following limits, if they exist.
   i. $\lim_{x \to 3} \sqrt{x^2 + 5x + 1}$
   ii. $\lim_{x \to 1} \cos(\pi x)$
   iii. $\lim_{x \to 2} \dfrac{2x + 4}{3x - 6}$
   iv. $\lim_{x \to \infty} \dfrac{x^2 - 4}{3x^2 + x + 7}$
   v. $\lim_{x \to 7} \dfrac{|x - 7|}{x - 7}$
   vi. $\lim_{x \to -2} \dfrac{x^2 - 4}{x + 2}$

(b) Explain why $\lim_{x \to 0} \dfrac{|x|}{x}$ does not exist, whereas $\lim_{x \to 0} \dfrac{x}{x}$ does exist.

(c) Using $\epsilon = 0.1$, find a value of δ that allows you to justify that $\lim_{x \to 3}(4x + 1) = 13$.

6. Answers to Sample Problems

(a) Find the following limits, if they exist.
   i. $\lim_{x \to 3} \sqrt{x^2 + 5x + 1} = 5$
   ii. $\lim_{x \to 1} \cos(\pi x) = -1$
   iii. $\lim_{x \to 2} \dfrac{2x + 4}{3x - 6}$ does not exist.
   iv. $\lim_{x \to \infty} \dfrac{x^2 - 4}{3x^2 + x + 7} = \lim_{x \to \infty} \dfrac{x^2 - 4}{3x^2 + x + 7} \left(\dfrac{\frac{1}{x^2}}{\frac{1}{x^2}} \right) = \lim_{x \to \infty} \dfrac{1 - \frac{4}{x^2}}{3 + \frac{1}{x} + \frac{7}{x^2}} = \dfrac{1}{3}.$

    v. $\lim\limits_{x \to 7} \dfrac{|x - 7|}{x - 7}$ does not exist. The fraction takes the value 1 if $x > 7$ and -1 if $x < 7$. So the limit does not exist. See (b) below for a similar example.

    vi. $\lim\limits_{x \to -2} \dfrac{x^2 - 4}{x + 2} = \lim\limits_{x \to -2} \dfrac{(x + 2)(x - 2)}{(x + 2)} = \lim\limits_{x \to -2} (x - 2) = -4.$

(b) Explain why $\lim\limits_{x \to 0} \dfrac{|x|}{x}$ does not exist, whereas $\lim\limits_{x \to 0} \dfrac{x}{x}$ does exist.

Examine what happens for values of x that are close to zero. If we pick a small positive value of x, then both expressions are equal to 1. This means that 1 might be the value of each limit. However, if we pick a negative value of x that happens to be close to zero (such as -0.001, for instance), then the first expression is equal to -1 while the second expression is equal to 1. To summarize, the first expression is equal to 1 for positive x-values and -1 for negative x-values. So $\frac{|x|}{x}$ does not have a limit as $x \to 0$. However, $\frac{x}{x} = 1$ for all positive and negative values of x. So it has a limit of 1 as $x \to 0$.

(c) Using $\epsilon = 0.1$, find a value of δ that allows you to justify that $\lim\limits_{x \to 3}(4x + 1) = 13$. Since the slope of this line is 4, we will choose $\delta = \frac{\epsilon}{4} = 0.025$. Thus, if $|x - 3| < 0.025$, then

$$
\begin{aligned}
-0.025 <\;\; & x - 3 \;\; < 0.025 \\
2.975 <\;\; & x \;\; < 3.025 \\
11.9 <\;\; & 4x \;\; < 12.1 \\
-0.1 <\;\; & 4x - 12 \;\; < 0.1,
\end{aligned}
$$

which means that $|4x + 1 - 13| < 0.1$, which is what we wanted.

b. Show that a polynomial function is continuous at a point

1. How do you show that polynomials are continuous at *every* real number?

To show continuity at $x = c$, we need to show that $\lim\limits_{x \to c} f(x) = f(c)$. The following example demonstrates how this can be done for polynomials. We will show that $f(x) = x^2 - 2x + 5$ is continuous at $x = 3$. Provide reasons for each equality.

$$
\begin{aligned}
\lim\limits_{x \to 3} f(x) &= \lim\limits_{x \to 3}(x^2 - 2x + 5) \\
&= \lim\limits_{x \to 3} x^2 - \lim\limits_{x \to 3} 2x + \lim\limits_{x \to 3} 5 \\
&= \left(\lim\limits_{x \to 3} x\right)^2 - 2\left(\lim\limits_{x \to 3} x\right) + \lim\limits_{x \to 3} 5 \\
&= (3)^2 - 2(3) + 5 \\
&= f(3).
\end{aligned}
$$

ANS: The reasons are (in order): definition of f, limit of a sum [respectively, difference] is the sum [resp., difference] of limits, limit of a product is the product of limits (and the limit of a constant is equal to that constant), $\lim\limits_{x \to 3} x = 3$, and the definition of f.

2. Sample Problems

(a) Find $\lim_{x \to 2}(x^7 - 4x^6 + x^5 + x^4 - 6x^2 - 7x + 12)$.

(b) Explain how you would show that ANY polynomial is continuous at any point.

(c) Is $f(x) = \dfrac{4x^3 - 4x + 1}{x^2 + 3}$ continuous at every point of its domain? Why or why not? [Hint: Can the denominator be zero?]

3. Answers to Sample Problems

(a) Find $\lim_{x \to 2}(x^7 - 4x^6 + x^5 + x^4 - 6x^2 - 7x + 12) = -106$.

(b) Explain how you would show that ANY polynomial is continuous at any point.

The steps in the example can be repeated for a general polynomial, $f(x)$. That is, the limit of the sum of terms is the sum of the limits of the individual terms. Then, the limit of x^n is just the n-th power of the limit of x. Finally, the limit of x as $x \to c$ is just c. So $\lim_{x \to c} f(x) = f(c)$, for any polynomial $f(x)$.

(c) Is $f(x) = \dfrac{4x^3 - 4x + 1}{x^2 + 3}$ continuous at every point of its domain? Why or why not? [Hint: Can the denominator be zero?] Since the denominator is always positive, there are no discontinuities in the domain of this rational function.

c. Apply the intermediate value theorem, using the geometric implications of continuity

1. What does the Intermediate Value Theorem say? How can you use geometry to demonstrate the Intermediate Value Theorem?

The Intermediate Value Theorem says that if f is continuous, then $f(x)$ attains every value in between $f(a)$ and $f(b)$. That is, if w is in the interval $[f(a), f(b)]$, then there exists at least one value c in the interval $[a, b]$ satisfying $f(c) = w$.

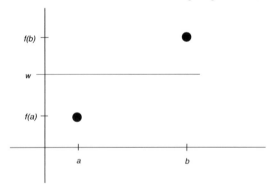

Geometrically speaking: No matter how you continuously connect $(a, f(a))$ to $(b, f(b))$, you must cross the line $y = w$ at least once.

2. What are some geometric implications of continuity?

My personal favorite is that the Intermediate Value Theorem can prove that, at any given time, there are two points on the Equator, directly opposite the earth from each other (antipodal points), that have the same temperature.

To see this, first, let $T(x)$ be the difference in temperature between the point on the equator that is x degrees east of $0°$ and the point $(x+180)$ degrees east of $0°$. [That is $T(x) = \text{temp}(x) - \text{temp}(x+180)$.] Suppose also that $T(0)$ is positive. Then $T(180)$ must be negative. Assuming temperature changes continuously, then there must be some value of c where $T(c) = 0$. See Sample Problems to fill in the missing details of the proof.

3. Sample Problems

   (a) Explain why $2x^4 - x - 21$ has to have a root between 1 and 2.

   (b) Suppose f is a polynomial, with $f(-2) = 6$, $f(0) = -3$, $f(1) = 1$, and $f(4) = 0$. What is the smallest possible degree of $f(x)$?

   (c) Fill in the details of the proof that there are antipodal points at the same temperature. For instance, what happens if $T(0) < 0$? How do you know for sure that $T(0)$ and $T(180)$ have different signs?

   (d) Show that there must be two antipodal points on the Equator which have the same relative humidity.

4. Answers to Sample Problems

   (a) Explain why $2x^4 - x - 21$ has to have a root between 1 and 2.
       $2(1)^4 - 1 - 21 = -6 < 0$, while $2(2)^4 - 2 - 21 = 9 > 0$. Since polynomials are continuous, the Intermediate Value Theorem says that this function must equal zero somewhere between 1 and 2.

   (b) Suppose f is a polynomial, with $f(-2) = 6$, $f(0) = -3$, $f(1) = 1$, and $f(4) = 0$. What is the smallest possible degree of $f(x)$? Three. We can deduce the existence of three zeroes, one between -2 and 0, one between 0 and 1, and one at 4.

   (c) Fill in the details of the proof that there are antipodal points at the same temperature. For instance, what happens if $T(0) < 0$? How do you know for sure that $T(0)$ and $T(180)$ have different signs?
       If $T(0) < 0$, then the argument is similar. In this case, $T(180)$ would be positive. So again, there must be a value of c for which $T(c) = 0$. Since 360 and 0 describe the same point, we have

$$T(180) = \text{temp}(180) - \text{temp}(360) = \text{temp}(180) - \text{temp}(0) = -T(0).$$

   So the signs of $T(0)$ and $T(180)$ have to be different. By the way, if $T(0)$ happens to equal zero, then $x = 0$ and $x = 180$ are the antipodal points at the same temperature.

   (d) Show that there must be two antipodal points on the Equator which have the same relative humidity.
       The proof is very similar to the proof regarding temperature. Simply replace "temperature" with "relative humidity."

5.3 Derivatives and Applications

a. Derive the rules of differentiation for polynomial, trigonometric, and logarithmic functions using the formal definition of derivative

1. What does the derivative represent?

   The derivative of f at $x = c$ represents the *instantaneous rate of change* of f at $x = c$. Graphically, the derivative represents the slope of the graph of $y = f(x)$ at $x = c$ (or the slope of the tangent line to $y = f(x)$ at $x = c$).

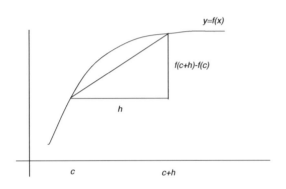
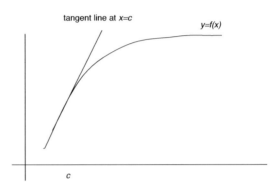

2. What is the formal definition of the derivative at a point?

   Finding the slope usually requires two points. (See left picture.) But to find the slope of a tangent line, you can find the slope between two points and then take the limit as those two points move closer toward each other. (See right picture.) Mathematically, the derivative of f at c is

   $$f'(c) = \lim_{h \to 0} \frac{f(c+h) - f(c)}{h}.$$

   There is an equivalent definition in the Sample Problems. Notice that the numerator and denominator BOTH approach zero, which means that we cannot calculate the limit just by plugging in $h = 0$ immediately. We have to be more thoughtful.

3. What is the formal definition of the derivative function?

   Next we can define a function $f'(x)$ whose value at $x = c$ is the slope of $f(x)$ at $x = c$. That is,

   $$f'(x) = \lim_{h \to 0} \frac{f(x+h) - f(x)}{h}.$$

   The derivative function can also be written as $\dfrac{df}{dx}$.

4. What are some properties of derivatives?

   One can show from the definition that the derivative of $kf(x)$ is $kf'(x)$ if k is a constant. One can also show:

   - the derivative of $f(x) \pm g(x)$ is $f'(x) \pm g'(x)$;

- the derivative of $f(x)g(x)$ is $f'(x)g(x) + f(x)g'(x)$ [Product Rule];
- the derivative of $\dfrac{f(x)}{g(x)}$ is $\dfrac{f'(x)g(x) - f(x)g'(x)}{g(x)^2}$ [Quotient Rule]; and
- the derivative of $f(g(x))$ is $f'(g(x))g'(x)$ [Chain Rule].

5. How do you use the definition to differentiate polynomial and trigonometric functions?

   Probably the most straightforward derivative examples are of the powers of x. As an example, let's find the derivative of $f(x) = x^2$ using the definition.

   $$f'(x) = \lim_{h \to 0} \frac{(x+h)^2 - x^2}{h} = \lim_{h \to 0} \frac{x^2 + 2xh + h^2 - x^2}{h} = \lim_{h \to 0}(2x + h) = 2x.$$

   Next we'll consider a trigonometric example. Let's find the derivative of $\sin x$ at $x = 0$.

   $$\lim_{h \to 0} \frac{\sin(0 + h) - \sin 0}{h} = \lim_{h \to 0} \frac{\sin h}{h} = 1.$$

   This means that the slope of the graph $y = \sin x$ is exactly 1 at $x = 0$ (WHEN x IS GIVEN IN RADIANS). [We'll see justification of this fact later, when we talk about L'Hôpital's Rule. You can also find proofs that utilize the "Squeeze Theorem," such as the brilliant online resource http://www.ies.co.jp/math/java/calc/LimSinX/LimSinX.html .]

6. How do you use the definition to differentiate logarithmic functions?

   Here's our plan:

   (a) Look at the derivative of an exponential function.

   (b) Figure out how the derivative of an inverse function relates to the derivative of the original function.

   (c) Find the derivative of a logarithmic function.

   Here we go:

   (a) Let's look at the exponential function $f(x) = e^x$. Its derivative is

   $$f'(x) = \lim_{h \to 0} \frac{e^{x+h} - e^x}{h} = \lim_{h \to 0} \frac{e^x e^h - e^x}{h} = e^x \left(\lim_{h \to 0} \frac{e^h - 1}{h} \right) = e^x.$$

   Yes, as $h \to 0$, the limit of $\frac{e^h - 1}{h}$ is 1. This is related to the fact that $e = \lim_{n \to \infty} \left(1 + \frac{1}{n} \right)^n$.

   (b) Next, consider $f^{-1}(x)$. Since the graph of $y = f^{-1}(x)$ is the same as the graph of $y = f(x)$ only reflected in the line $y = x$, the slopes at corresponding points are reciprocals of each other (because $\frac{\Delta y}{\Delta x}$ becomes $\frac{\Delta x}{\Delta y}$).

   (c) So, the derivative of $y = \ln x$ at $x = 2$, say, is the reciprocal of the derivative of $y = e^x$ at $y = 2$ (and $x = \ln 2$). Since the derivative of $f(x) = e^x$ is $f'(x) = e^x$, its slope at $\ln 2$ is 2. So the derivative of $\ln x$ at 2 is $\frac{1}{2}$. Similarly, the slope of $y = \ln x$ at $x = c > 0$ is $\frac{1}{c}$. Therefore, the derivative function of $y = \ln x$ is $y' = \frac{1}{x}$.

7. What is implicit differentiation? ...logarithmic differentiation?

Implicit differentiation can be used to find $\dfrac{dy}{dx}$ when y is an implicit function of x. The idea is to take the derivative as usual, but remember that y is a function of x, and so it requires the Chain Rule to be properly differentiated. For example, to find the slope of the circle $x^2 + y^2 = 5$ at the point $(-1, -2)$, we can use implicit differentiation.

$$x^2 + y^2 = 5 \Rightarrow 2x + 2y\frac{dy}{dx} = 0 \Rightarrow \frac{dy}{dx} = -\frac{x}{y}.$$

So, at $(-1, -2)$, we have $\dfrac{dy}{dx} = -\dfrac{1}{2}$.

Sometimes, one has to take a logarithm of both sides first, which leads some people to use the term "logarithmic differentiation." See Sample Problems for an example.

8. Sample Problems

   (a) Find a formula for the derivative of $y = 3x^2 + x$ using the formal definition.

   (b) Show that the derivative of x^n is nx^{n-1}.

   (c) Using the definition of the derivative, find the derivative of $\dfrac{1}{x}$ and of $\dfrac{1}{x^2}$.

   (d) Use the Product Rule to find the derivative of $x^2 = x \cdot x$.

   (e) Use the Quotient Rule to find the derivative of $\tan x = \dfrac{\sin x}{\cos x}$.

   (f) Use the Chain Rule to find the derivative of $\sin(3x^2)$ and $\ln(1 + x^2)$.

   (g) Another way to define the derivative of f at $x = c$ is

   $$f'(c) = \lim_{b \to c} \frac{f(b) - f(c)}{b - c}.$$

   Explain why this definition is equivalent to the one given above. Draw a picture showing your reasoning.

   (h) Using the alternate definition of the derivative, find derivatives of x^2 and $\frac{1}{x}$.

   (i) Using the definition of the derivative, find the derivative of $y = \cos x$. You may use the fact that $\lim\limits_{h \to 0} \dfrac{\sin h}{h} = 1$ and $\lim\limits_{h \to 0} \dfrac{\cos h - 1}{h} = 0$.

   (j) Find the derivative of $y = x^x$. [Hint: Use logarithmic differentiation by taking the logarithm of both sides and then implicitly differentiating the resulting equation.]

9. Answers to Sample Problems

   (a) Find a formula for the derivative of $y = 3x^2 + x$ using the formal definition.

   $$\begin{aligned} f'(x) &= \lim_{h \to 0} \frac{3(x + h)^2 + (x + h) - (3x^2 + x)}{h} \\ &= \lim_{h \to 0} \frac{3x^2 + 6xh + 3h^2 + x + h - 3x^2 - x}{h} \\ &= \lim_{h \to 0} \frac{6xh + 3h^2 + h}{h} = \lim_{h \to 0}(6x + 3h + 1) = 6x + 1. \end{aligned}$$

(b) Show that the derivative of x^n is nx^{n-1}. Using the formal definition (and the Binomial Theorem), we get:

$$
\begin{aligned}
f'(x) &= \lim_{h\to 0} \frac{(x+h)^n - x^n}{h} \\
&= \lim_{h\to 0} \frac{\left[x^n + \binom{n}{1} x^{n-1}h + \binom{n}{2} x^{n-2}h^2 + \ldots\right] - x^n}{h} \\
&= \lim_{h\to 0} \frac{nx^{n-1}h + \frac{n(n-1)}{2}x^{n-2}h^2 + \ldots}{h} \\
&= \lim_{h\to 0} \left[nx^{n-1} + \frac{n(n-1)}{2}x^{n-2}h + \ldots\right] = nx^{n-1}.
\end{aligned}
$$

Notice that all the unwritten terms have a factor of h. So, they go to zero as $h \to 0$.

(c) Using the definition of the derivative, find the derivative of $\frac{1}{x}$ and of $\frac{1}{x^2}$.

$$
\lim_{h\to 0} \frac{\frac{1}{x+h} - \frac{1}{x}}{h} = \lim_{h\to 0} \frac{\frac{x-(x+h)}{x(x+h)}}{h} = \lim_{h\to 0} \frac{-h}{hx(x+h)} = \lim_{h\to 0} \frac{-1}{x(x+h)} = -\frac{1}{x^2}, \text{ and}
$$

$$
\lim_{h\to 0} \frac{\frac{1}{(x+h)^2} - \frac{1}{x^2}}{h} = \lim_{h\to 0} \frac{x^2 - (x+h)^2}{hx^2(x+h)^2} = \lim_{h\to 0} \frac{-2xh - h^2}{hx^2(x+h)^2} = \lim_{h\to 0} \frac{-2x - h}{x^2(x+h)^2} = -\frac{2}{x^3}.
$$

(d) Use the Product Rule to find the derivative of $x^2 = x \cdot x$.

Since $f(x) = g(x) = x$, we find that the derivative of x^2 is $(1)(x) + (x)(1) = 2x$.

(e) Use the Quotient Rule to find the derivative of $\tan x = \frac{\sin x}{\cos x}$.

$$
\frac{d}{dx}\left(\frac{\sin x}{\cos x}\right) = \frac{\cos x \cos x - (\sin x)(-\sin x)}{\cos^2 x} = \frac{\cos^2 x + \sin^2 x}{\cos^2 x} = \frac{1}{\cos^2 x} = \sec^2 x
$$

(f) Use the Chain Rule to find the derivative of $\sin(3x^2)$ and $\ln(1+x^2)$.

The derivative of $\sin(3x^2)$ is $(\cos(3x^2))(6x) = 6x\cos(3x^2)$.

The derivative of $\ln(1+x^2)$ is $\frac{1}{1+x^2}(2x) = \frac{2x}{1+x^2}$.

(g) Another way to define the derivative of f at $x = c$ is

$$
f'(c) = \lim_{b\to c} \frac{f(b) - f(c)}{b - c}.
$$

Explain why this definition is equivalent to the one given above. Draw a picture showing your reasoning.

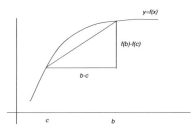

Both definitions lead to the instantaneous rate of change at the point $x = c$. In fact, by letting $b = c + h$, the two definitions are exactly the same.

(h) Using the alternate definition of the derivative, find derivatives of x^2 and $\frac{1}{x}$.

$$\lim_{b \to c} \frac{b^2 - c^2}{b - c} = \lim_{b \to c} \frac{(b + c)(b - c)}{b - c} = \lim_{b \to c} (b + c) = 2c, \text{ and}$$

$$\lim_{b \to c} \frac{\frac{1}{b} - \frac{1}{c}}{b - c} = \lim_{b \to c} \frac{\frac{c-b}{bc}}{b - c} = \lim_{b \to c} \frac{-1}{bc} = -\frac{1}{c^2}.$$

(i) Using the definition of the derivative, find the derivative of $y = \cos x$. You may use the fact that $\lim_{h \to 0} \frac{\sin h}{h} = 1$ and $\lim_{h \to 0} \frac{\cos h - 1}{h} = 0$.

$$\begin{aligned}
\lim_{h \to 0} \frac{\cos(x + h) - \cos x}{h} &= \lim_{h \to 0} \frac{\cos x \cos h - \sin x \sin h - \cos x}{h} \\
&= \lim_{h \to 0} \frac{\cos x (\cos h - 1) - \sin x \sin h}{h} \\
&= \cos x \left(\lim_{h \to 0} \frac{\cos h - 1}{h} \right) - \sin x \left(\lim_{h \to 0} \frac{\sin h}{h} \right) \\
&= (\cos x)(0) - (\sin x)(1) = -\sin x.
\end{aligned}$$

(j) Find the derivative of $y = x^x$. [Hint: Use logarithmic differentiation by taking the logarithm of both sides and then implicitly differentiating the resulting equation.]

$$y = x^x \Rightarrow \ln y = \ln x^x = x \ln x \Rightarrow \frac{1}{y} \frac{dy}{dx} = 1 \ln x + x \left(\frac{1}{x} \right) = \ln x + 1,$$

which means that $\frac{dy}{dx} = y(\ln x + 1) = x^x(\ln x + 1)$. Notice that we used a property of logarithms and the Product Rule.

b. Interpret the concept of derivative geometrically, numerically, and analytically (i.e., slope of the tangent, limit of difference quotients, extrema, Newton's method, and instantaneous rate of change)

1. How is the concept of the derivative related to its definition?

   The derivative represents an instantaneous rate of change of a function f. This is reflected in the definition because to find an instantaneous rate of change, you need to compute a rate of change between two points and then examine what happens as the second point approaches the first.

2. What does the derivative mean geometrically? ...numerically? ...analytically?

   Geometrically, the derivative of f at $x = c$ is equal to the slope of the tangent line to $y = f(x)$ at $x = c$. Numerically, this can be approximated by taking the slope between two points that are very close to each other: one at $x = c$ and one very close to c (at $c + h$ for small *h*). For most functions, the closer the second point is to the first, the better the numerical approximation will be. Analytically, one needs to examine the difference quotient (slope, rate of change) of the function f between the x-values of c and $c + h$ and determine the limit of this quotient as $h \to 0$. This is precisely the definition of $f'(c)$.

3. What is Newton's Method? How is it used?

   Newton's Method uses tangent lines to estimate roots of a function. (See picture below.) Suppose you can't solve $f(x) = 0$ exactly. Then you can make a guess: x_0. Using this guess, construct the tangent line to $y = f(x)$ at x_0. Then determine where this tangent line crosses the x-axis, say at x_1. (You can always find the x-intercept of a non-horizontal line.) Then you can either use x_1 as your guess for the solution or you can repeat the process. Construct the tangent line at x_1 and then determine where the line meets the x-axis, at x_2. Continue until you are as close to the solution of $f(x) = 0$ as you wish.

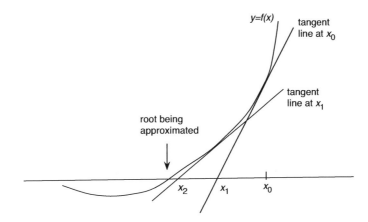

   The formula (which can be deduced from the explanation above – see Sample Problems) for x_{n+1} in terms of x_n is:

   $$x_{n+1} = x_n - \frac{f(x_n)}{f'(x_n)}.$$

4. Sample Problems

   (a) Find the equation of the tangent line to $y = 3x^3$ at the point $x = 2$.

   (b) Find the equation of the tangent line to $y = \frac{6}{x^2}$ at the point $x = 1$.

   (c) Referring to the graphs of $y = \sin x$ and $y = \cos x$, explain why the derivative of $\sin x$ is $\cos x$ and the derivative of $\cos x$ is $-\sin x$.

   (d) Using the data in the table, find a good estimate for $f'(3)$.

x	1	2	3	4
$f(x)$	5	4	2	-1

   (e) Using Newton's Method, estimate the root of $x^2 - 3$ that lies between 1 and 2. [Review: How do you know there *is* a root between 1 and 2?]

   (f) Deduce the Newton's Method formula. Find the tangent line at x_0 and then find x_1, its x-intercept.

5. Answers to Sample Problems

(a) Find the equation of the tangent line to $y = 3x^3$ at the point $x = 2$.

The tangent line is $y = 36x - 48$.

(b) Find the equation of the tangent line to $y = \frac{6}{x^2}$ at the point $x = 1$.

The tangent line is $y = -12x + 18$.

(c) Referring to the graphs of $y = \sin x$ and $y = \cos x$, explain why the derivative of $\sin x$ is $\cos x$ and the derivative of $\cos x$ is $-\sin x$.

Notice that the slope of $\sin x$ at zero is a positive number. As x increases, the slope of $\sin x$ becomes zero, then negative, then zero again, and then positive again at 2π. If we are in radians, then the maximum slope of $\sin x$ (at $x = 0$) is 1, which is $\cos 0$. So it's not hard to believe that the derivative of $\sin x$ is $\cos x$.

Similarly, at $x = 0$, the slope of $\cos x$ is zero. As x increases, the slopes become negative, then zero, then positive, then zero again at 2π. This is the opposite behavior of the sine function. So it's not hard to believe that the derivative of $\cos x$ is $-\sin x$.

(d) Using the data in the table, find a good estimate for $f'(3)$.

x	1	2	3	4
$f(x)$	5	4	2	-1

To find the best estimate we can, we will use the smallest interval possible from the given data, which is $\Delta x = 1$. Also, we will average the slopes to the left and to the right of 3. To the left, we get $\frac{f(3)-f(2)}{3-2} = \frac{2-4}{1} = -2$, and to the right, we get $\frac{f(4)-f(3)}{4-3} = -3$. So we will guess $f'(3) = -2.5$. Notice that this is the same result you get when you find the slope between 2 and 4. That is, $\frac{f(4)-f(2)}{4-2} = \frac{-1-4}{2} = -2.5$.

(e) Using Newton's Method, estimate the root of $x^2 - 3$ that lies between 1 and 2. [Review: How do you know there *is* a root between 1 and 2?] We know there is a root between 1 and 2 because of the Intermediate Value Theorem: $f(1) = -2 < 0$ and $f(2) = 1 > 0$. To find it, we start with a guess. You can use anything between 1 and 2, but I'll start with $x_0 = \frac{3}{2}$. Notice that we need $f(x) = x^2 - 3$ and $f'(x) = 2x$ in the formula. So

$$x_1 = x_0 - \frac{f(x_0)}{f'(x_0)} = \frac{3}{2} - \frac{\frac{9}{4} - 3}{2(\frac{3}{2})} = \frac{3}{2} - \frac{\frac{-3}{4}}{3} = \frac{3}{2} + \frac{1}{4} = \frac{7}{4}; \text{ and}$$

$$x_2 = \frac{7}{4} - \frac{\frac{49}{16} - 3}{2(\frac{7}{4})} = \frac{7}{4} - \frac{\frac{1}{16}}{\frac{7}{2}} = \frac{7}{4} - \frac{1}{56} = \frac{97}{56}$$

This will be fine, especially since there are no calculators on this part of the CSET! $(\frac{97}{56})^2 = \frac{9409}{3136} = 3 + \frac{1}{3136} \approx 3.00032$, which is pretty close to 3.

(f) Deduce the Newton's Method formula. Find the tangent line at x_0 and then find x_1, its x-intercept.

To find the tangent line to $f(x)$ at x_0, we need to know the point of tangency: $(x_0, f(x_0))$ and the slope at that point: $f'(x_0)$. Using the point-slope form of the line, we know that the tangent line is $y - f(x_0) = f'(x_0)(x - x_0)$. The x-intercept x_1 of this line occurs when $y = 0$. So

$$0 - f(x_0) = f'(x_0)(x_1 - x_0) \Rightarrow -\frac{f(x_0)}{f'(x_0)} = x_1 - x_0 \Rightarrow x_1 = x_0 - \frac{f(x_0)}{f'(x_0)}.$$

This procedure works at each and every step, which means $x_{n+1} = x_n - \frac{f(x_n)}{f'(x_n)}$.

c. Interpret both continuous and differentiable functions geometrically and analytically and apply Rolle's theorem, the mean value theorem, and L'Hôpital's rule

1. What's the difference between "continuous" and "differentiable" functions?

   A function is called "differentiable" at a point if its derivative is continuous at that point. It can be shown that ALL FUNCTIONS THAT ARE DIFFERENTIABLE EVERYWHERE ARE CONTINUOUS EVERYWHERE. However, not all continuous functions are differentiable. Functions with cusps, corners, and vertical tangents are not differentiable at those points.

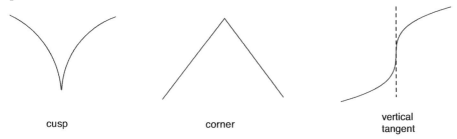

cusp   corner   vertical
                                                  tangent

   Analytically, this means that the limit given in the definition of the derivative does not exist at the point in question. There are two main reasons why the derivative would not exist. Either there is no unique tangent line at the point in question, or the slope of the tangent line is undefined.

2. What does Rolle's Theorem say? How do you interpret it geometrically and analytically?

   Rolle's Theorem: If f is continuous on $[a, b]$ and differentiable on (a, b), and if $f(a) = f(b)$, then there is some number c between a and b satisfying $f'(c) = 0$.

   Geometrically, this means that if you start and end a continuous and differentiable function at the same y-value, then you must have turned around (switched from increasing to decreasing or vice versa) at some point. Analytically, Rolle's Theorem means that because there must be a local maximum or local minimum value of the function f on the interval (a, b), then $f'(x)$ must equal zero somewhere on the interval (a, b). In the picture below, there are three possible choices for c.

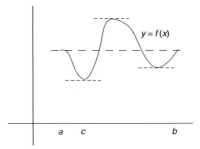

3. What does the Mean Value Theorem say? How do you interpret it geometrically and analytically?

   Mean Value Theorem: If f is continuous on $[a, b]$ and differentiable on (a, b), then there is some number c between a and b satisfying

   $$f'(c) = \frac{f(b) - f(a)}{b - a}.$$

   Geometrically, this means that there is some point where the slope of the tangent line of f is equal to the slope between the starting and ending points of f.

   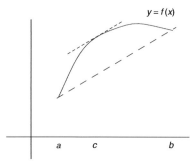

   To prove the Mean Value Theorem analytically, we can subtract the line through $(a, f(a))$ and $(b, f(b))$ from the function $f(x)$ to get a function $g(x)$ which satisfies all the conditions of Rolle's Theorem. Then the value of c making $g'(c) = 0$ is the same value of c making $f'(c) = \frac{f(b)-f(a)}{b-a}$. See Sample Problems.

4. What does L'Hôpital's Rule say? How do you interpret it geometrically and analytically?

   L'Hôpital's Rule is used to evaluate certain limits which cannot be determined at first glance. If you are evaluating a limit of a quotient, and the quotient is "indeterminate," meaning that it is approaching $\frac{\infty}{\infty}$ or $\frac{0}{0}$, then more information is needed. In these cases (and only in these cases)

   $$\lim_{x \to c} \frac{f(x)}{g(x)} = \lim_{x \to c} \frac{f'(x)}{g'(x)}.$$

   For example, $\displaystyle\lim_{x \to 1} \frac{x - 1}{\ln x} \to \frac{0}{0}$, and thus

   $$\lim_{x \to 1} \frac{x - 1}{\ln x} = \lim_{x \to 1} \frac{1}{1/x} = 1.$$

5. Sample Problems

   (a) L'Hôpital's Rule works for limits as $x \to \infty$ as well. Write down L'Hôpital's Rule in this case.

   (b) Evaluate these limits. If they do not exist, write "DNE."

   i. $\displaystyle\lim_{x \to \infty} \frac{x}{e^x}$

    ii. $\lim\limits_{x \to 0} \dfrac{\cos x - 1}{x^2}$

(c) Verify that $\lim\limits_{x \to 0} \dfrac{\sin x}{x} = 1$.

(d) How do you know that the *derivative* of $\cos 2x$ has a root between 0 and π?

(e) Explain how Rolle's Theorem is a special case of the Mean Value Theorem.

(f) Apply the Mean Value Theorem to the function x^2 between 0 and 1 to complete the sentence: There must be a point c between 0 and 1 satisfying $f'(c) = \ldots$. Find the point.

(g) Fill in details of the Mean Value Theorem proof.

6. Answers to Sample Problems

(a) L'Hôpital's Rule works for limits as $x \to \infty$ as well. Write down L'Hôpital's Rule in this case.

If $\lim\limits_{x \to \infty} \dfrac{f(x)}{g(x)} \to \dfrac{0}{0}$ or $\pm \dfrac{\infty}{\infty}$, then $\lim\limits_{x \to \infty} \dfrac{f(x)}{g(x)} = \lim\limits_{x \to \infty} \dfrac{f'(x)}{g'(x)}$.

(b) Evaluate these limits. If they do not exist, write "DNE."

    i. $\lim\limits_{x \to \infty} \dfrac{x}{e^x} \left(\to \dfrac{0}{0} \right) = \lim\limits_{x \to \infty} \dfrac{1}{e^x} = 0$

    ii. $\lim\limits_{x \to 0} \dfrac{\cos x - 1}{x^2} \left(\to \dfrac{0}{0} \right) = \lim\limits_{x \to 0} \dfrac{-\sin x}{2x} \left(\to \dfrac{0}{0} \right) = \lim\limits_{x \to 0} \dfrac{-\cos x}{2} = -\dfrac{1}{2}$

(c) Verify that $\lim\limits_{x \to 0} \dfrac{\sin x}{x} = 1$. Using L'Hôpital's Rule, we get

$$\lim\limits_{x \to 0} \dfrac{\sin x}{x} = \lim\limits_{x \to 0} \dfrac{\cos x}{1} = 1.$$

(d) How do you know that the *derivative* of $\cos 2x$ has a root between 0 and π?

Since $\cos(2(0)) = \cos(2\pi) = 1$, Rolle's Theorem says that the derivative of $\cos 2x$ must be zero at some point between 0 and π.

(e) Explain how Rolle's Theorem is a special case of the Mean Value Theorem.

If we apply the Mean Value Theorem in the special case where $f(a) = f(b)$, then the Mean Value Theorem says that there is a point c between a and b satisfying $f'(c) = \dfrac{f(b)-f(a)}{b-a} = 0$. This is precisely Rolle's Theorem.

(f) Apply the Mean Value Theorem to the function x^2 between 0 and 1 to complete the sentence: There must be a point c between 0 and 1 satisfying $f'(c) = \ldots$. Find the point.

There must be a point c between 0 and 1 satisfying $f'(c) = \dfrac{1^2 - 0^2}{1-0} = 1$. Since $f'(x) = 2x$, we can deduce that $c = \dfrac{1}{2}$.

(g) Fill in details of the Mean Value Theorem proof.

The explanation given above says to subtract the line through $(a, f(a))$ and $(b, f(b))$ from $f(x)$. Explicitly, this line is $y - f(a) = m(x - a)$, where $m = \frac{f(b)-f(a)}{b-a}$. (There are other valid formulas.) So,

$$g(x) = f(x) - [f(a) + m(x - a)] = f(x) - f(a) - \frac{f(b) - f(a)}{b - a}(x - a).$$

Notice that $g(a) = f(a) - f(a) - 0 = 0$ and that $g(b) = f(b) - f(a) - (f(b) - f(a)) = 0$. So, applying Rolle's Theorem to $g(x)$, we know that there must be a value c between a and b satisfying $g'(c) = 0$. But $g'(x) = f'(x) - \frac{f(b)-f(a)}{b-a}$. So, if $g'(c) = 0$, then $f'(c) = \frac{f(b)-f(a)}{b-a}$, which is what we wanted to show. $\square$

d. Use the derivative to solve rectilinear motion, related rate, and optimization problems

1. **What is rectilinear motion? How can you use the derivative to solve problems?**

   Rectilinear motion will mean motion along a straight line. The derivative can be used to describe velocity (and the second derivative, acceleration) of a particle if you know the particle's position as a function of time. For instance, if a particle's x-coordinate at time t (in seconds) is $16t^2$ feet, then its velocity is $32t$ feet per second and its acceleration is 32 feet per second per second.

2. **What is meant by "related rates?" How can you use the derivative to solve problems?**

   If two quantities are related by an equation, then their rates of change (derivatives) are also related. Let's look at a sample question: Suppose you are 6 feet tall and you are walking toward a 15 foot tall streetlight at a constant rate of 2 feet per second. How fast is the length of your shadow changing when you are 10 feet from the base of the streetlight? To solve this, we need to relate the length of the shadow to the distance from you to the lamppost. Then we take derivatives to determine the relationship between the given rates of change. So, let x represent your distance to the lamppost and let s be the length of your shadow.

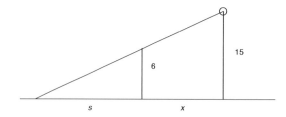

   Using similar triangles (or trigonometry), we get $\frac{s}{6} = \frac{x+s}{15}$ or $15s = 6x + 6s$, which means that $s = \frac{2}{3}x$. So, by taking derivatives, we must have $\frac{ds}{dt} = \frac{2}{3}\frac{dx}{dt} = \frac{2}{3}(2) = \frac{4}{3}$ feet per second. So, when you are 10 feet from the lamppost, or at any point, the length of your shadow is changing at a rate of about 1.333 feet per second.

3. **How do you use the derivative to optimize a function?**

If you are trying to optimize a function, then you need to check the places where the derivative is zero or undefined (such as at endpoints of your allowed region). For example, suppose we want to maximize the revenue function $R(x) = 24x - x^2$, where $0 \leq x \leq 24$. We first find the derivative $R'(x) = 24 - 2x$ and set it equal to zero, obtaining $x = 12$. So our critical points (see the next section on maxima and minima) are $x = 0$, 12, and 24. Checking these gives $R(0) = R(24) = 0$, whereas $R(12) = 144$. So the revenue function is optimized when $x = 12$.

4. Sample Problems

   (a) A particle moves up and down on the surface of the water so that its height as a function of time is $\sin t$. Find its velocity.

   (b) The standard formula for the height of a projectile on Earth is $h(t) = h_0 + v_0 t - 16t^2$, where t is in seconds, h_0 is the initial height in feet, and v_0 is the initial upward velocity in feet per second.

      i. Show that $h(0) = h_0$ by plugging in $t = 0$.

      ii. Show that $v(0) = v_0$ by taking the derivative of $h(t)$ to find $v(t)$.

      iii. Show that the acceleration due to gravity is constant (by taking the derivative of $v(t)$). What is the value of the acceleration due to gravity on Earth? Give units.

   (c) In the related rates example, how fast is the tip of your shadow moving toward the lamppost? [Hint: find out how fast $x + s$ is changing.]

   (d) Sand falls at a constant rate of 20mm^3 per second through an hourglass, forming a cone-shaped pile that has a slant angle of $\pi/4$. How fast is the height of the pile changing when the height of the pile is 10mm?

   (e) Find the maximum height reached by an object fired upward from the ground with a velocity of 96 feet per second. [Use the formula above.]

   (f) Repeat the previous problem, but use an initial velocity of v_0.

5. Answers to Sample Problems

   (a) A particle moves up and down on the surface of the water so that its height as a function of time is $\sin t$. Find its velocity. $\cos t$

   (b) The standard formula for the height of a projectile on Earth is $h(t) = h_0 + v_0 t - 16t^2$, where t is in seconds, h_0 is the initial height in feet, and v_0 is the initial upward velocity in feet per second.

      i. Show that $h(0) = h_0$ by plugging in $t = 0$. $h(0) = h_0 + 0 - 0 = h_0$

      ii. Show that $v(0) = v_0$ by taking the derivative of $h(t)$ to find $v(t)$. $v(t) = h'(t) = v_0 - 32t$. So $v(0) = v_0 - 0 = v_0$.

      iii. Show that the acceleration due to gravity is constant (by taking the derivative of $v(t)$). What is the value of the acceleration due to gravity on Earth? Give units. $a(t) = v'(t) = -32$. The acceleration due to gravity of Earth is approximately 32 feet per second per second downward.

(c) In the related rates example, how fast is the tip of your shadow moving toward the lamppost? [Hint: find out how fast $x + s$ is changing.]

$$\frac{d(x+s)}{dt} = \frac{dx}{dt} + \frac{ds}{dt} = 2 + \frac{4}{3} = \frac{10}{3}.$$

So the tip of your shadow is moving toward the lamppost at a rate of $\frac{10}{3}$ feet per second.

(d) Sand falls at a constant rate of 20mm^3 per second through an hourglass, forming a cone-shaped pile that has a slant angle of $\pi/4$. How fast is the height of the pile changing when the height of the pile is 10mm?

This is a classic related rates problem. The slant angle of $\pi/4$ means that the cone's height is equal to its radius. Since the volume of a cone in general is $\frac{1}{3}\pi r^2 h$, then the volume of our cone is $V = \frac{1}{3}\pi h^3$. We are told that $\frac{dV}{dt} = 20$. So, taking the derivative with respect to t, we get

$$\frac{dV}{dt} = \pi h^2 \frac{dh}{dt} \Rightarrow 20 = \pi(10)^2 \frac{dh}{dt} \Rightarrow \frac{dh}{dt} = \frac{1}{5\pi}.$$

Thus, when the height of the pile is 10mm, the height of the pile is increasing at a rate of $\frac{1}{5\pi}$ mm per second.

(e) Find the maximum height reached by an object fired upward from the ground with a velocity of 96 feet per second. [Use the formula above.] The height is given by $h(t) = 0 + 96t - 16t^2$. So, to maximize the height, we find when $h'(t) = 0$ (i.e., zero velocity). $h'(t) = 96 - 32t = 0$ implies $t = 3$ seconds. The maximum height is thus $h(3) = 96(3) - 16(3)^2 = 288 - 144 = 144$ feet.

(f) Repeat the previous problem, but use an initial velocity of v_0.

$$h'(t) = v_0 - 32t = 0 \Rightarrow t = \frac{v_0}{32}$$

So, the maximum height is thus $h(\frac{v_0}{32}) = v_0(\frac{v_0}{32}) - 16(\frac{v_0}{32})^2 = \frac{v_0^2}{64}$ feet.

e. Use the derivative to analyze functions and planar curves (e.g., maxima, minima, inflection points, concavity)

1. What are maxima and minima? How do you find them?

An x-value p is called a *local maximum* of f if $f(x) \leq f(p)$ for all values of x near p. The definition of a local minimum is similar. (See Sample Problems.) Local maxima and minima must occur at critical points of f; that is, points c where $f'(c)$ is either zero or undefined (such as at endpoints of the domain).

2. What is concavity?

Concavity describes the direction of curvature of the graph of f. We say f is concave up if it is shaped like a bowl (or like $y = x^2$, opening upward), and concave down if the graph of f is shaped like a dome (or like $y = -x^2$, opening downward). Straight lines have no concavity.

3. What are inflection points? How do you find them?

An inflection point is a point where the graph of the function f changes its concavity - which means that $f''(x)$ changes sign at these points. This occurs at critical points of f'; that is, points where $f''(x)$ is either zero or undefined.

4. How do you graph a function if you know maxima, minima, inflection points, and concavity?

These help you find important points on the function, and can tell you important features of the graph. Let's do an example: $y = x^3 - 3x$.

First, we take derivatives. If $f(x) = x^3 - 3x$, then $f'(x) = 3x^2 - 3$ and $f''(x) = 6x$. To find critical points, we set $f'(x) = 0$. Then $3x^2 - 3 = 0$, which means that there are two critical points, $x = \pm 1$. [Using $f'(-2) = f'(2) = 9$ and $f'(0) = -3$, we see that slopes of f are positive for $x < -1$, then negative from $x = -1$ to $x = 1$, then positive again for $x > 1$.] So, -1 is a local maximum and 1 is a local minimum. Let's plot $(1, f(1))$ and $(-1, f(-1))$ on the graph of f. Setting $f''(x) = 0$, we find that $x = 0$ is a possible inflection point. Checking that indeed, $f''(x)$ changes from negative to positive at $x = 0$, then 0 is an inflection point. In fact $f(x)$ changes from concave down to concave up at that point. Plot $(0, f(0))$ on the graph as well. Now, we can also find zeroes of this function: $0 = x(x^2 - 3)$, which means $x = 0, \pm\sqrt{3}$ are zeroes of $f(x)$. Plotting all these important points, combined with our knowledge of end behavior as $x \to \pm\infty$, we get a graph of $y = f(x)$.

y=x^3-3x

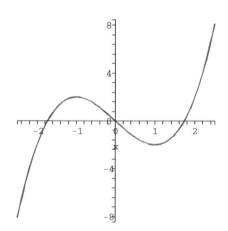

5. Sample Problems

   (a) Find local maxima and minima and inflection points of the following functions.
       i. $x^4 - 2x^2$
       ii. $x^3 - 3x^2 + 2x$
       iii. e^x
       iv. $\sin x$ on $[0, 2\pi]$

   (b) Sketch a graph of $y = x^4 - 2x^2$, labeling important points.

   (c) TRUE or FALSE. Explain.

    i. If f is increasing, then f' is positive.

    ii. If f' is concave up, then f is increasing.

    iii. If f is concave up, then f'' is increasing.

    iv. If $f'' > 0$, then f' is increasing and f is concave up.

    v. If $f' > 0$, then $f > 0$.

(d) Define what it means for p to be a *local minimum* of f.

6. Answers to Sample Problems

(a) Find local maxima and minima and inflection points of the following functions.

    i. $x^4 - 2x^2$ maximum: 0, minima: -1 and 1, inflection: $\pm\frac{1}{\sqrt{3}}$

    ii. $x^3 - 3x^2 + 2x$ maximum: $1 - \frac{\sqrt{3}}{3}$, minimum: $1 + \frac{\sqrt{3}}{3}$, inflection: 1

    iii. e^x no maxima, no minima, and no inflection points

    iv. $\sin x$ on $[0, 2\pi]$ maximum: $\frac{\pi}{2}$, minimum: $\frac{3\pi}{2}$, inflection: 0, π, and 2π.

(b) Sketch a graph of $y = x^4 - 2x^2$, labeling important points.

Maxima, minima, and inflection points were found above. There are also zeroes at 0, $-\sqrt{2}$, and $\sqrt{2}$.

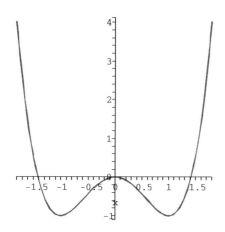

y=x^4-2x^2

(c) TRUE or FALSE. Explain.

    i. If f is increasing, then f' is positive. TRUE. An increasing function has a positive slope.

    ii. If f' is concave up, then f is increasing. FALSE. f' could be concave up and negative, which would mean that f would be decreasing. The concavity of f' does not relate to whether or not f is increasing.

    iii. If f is concave up, then f'' is increasing. FALSE. If f is concave up, then we know f'' is positive, but it might not be increasing.

    iv. If $f'' > 0$, then f' is increasing and f is concave up. TRUE. f' increases precisely when f'' is positive, and when f is concave up.

    v. If $f' > 0$, then $f > 0$. FALSE. If $f' > 0$, then f is increasing. But that does not mean that f has to take positive values.

(d) Define what it means for p to be a *local minimum* of f.

    An x-value p is called a *local minimum* of f if $f(x) \geq f(p)$ for all values of x near p.

f. Solve separable first-order differential equations and apply them to growth and decay problems

1. What is a differential equation?

   A differential equation is one which involves functions and their derivatives. To solve a differential equation means to find the function whose derivatives satisfy the given equation. For example, $y = e^x$ is a solution to the differential equation $\dfrac{dy}{dx} = y$ because $\dfrac{dy}{dx} = e^x = y$.

2. What is a separable, first-order differential equation? How do you solve them?

   A separable, first-order differential equation is one which can be solved by (artificially) separating the dy and dx of the derivative so that all the x terms wind up on one side (with dx) and all the y terms wind up on the other side (with dy). "First-order" means that only the first derivative of y is involved. You can solve a first-order separable equation by separating the variables and integrating each side. This might be a topic for the next section (Integrals), but occasionally you can guess the answer and check it, using only your knowledge of derivatives.

3. How do growth and decay problems relate to separable first-order differential equations? How do you solve growth and decay problems?

   Exponential growth and decay arises mathematically from differential equations. For instance, let's suppose that a population P grows at a rate that is proportional to the population. (This makes sense because maybe a certain percentage of the population is reproducing at any time.) Then $\dfrac{dP}{dt} = kP$, where k is a constant. The solution to this equation is $P(t) = P_0 e^{kt}$, where P_0 represents the initial population, $P(0)$. So, whenever the growth rate is proportional to the population, one has exponential growth. Similarly, if the decay rate is proportional to the amount remaining, then one obtains exponential decay.

4. Sample Problems

   (a) Show that $y = 5e^{-2t}$ is a solution to $\dfrac{dy}{dt} = -2y$.

   (b) Show that $y = Ae^{-kt}$ is a solution to $\dfrac{dy}{dt} = -ky$.

   (c) Show that $y = 3x^2$ is a solution to $\dfrac{dy}{dx} = \dfrac{2y}{x}$.

   (d) Show that $y = Ax^3$ is a solution to $\dfrac{dy}{dx} = \dfrac{3y}{x}$.

   (e) Solve $\dfrac{dy}{dx} = \cos x$.

(f) Suppose that a population of bacteria grows at a rate proportional to its population, and assume that the constant of proportionality is 0.5hr^{-1}. Write down a differential equation stating this assumption. Solve it, assuming that the initial population is 4000 bacteria. Find the doubling time for this population.

(g) The quantity $Q(t)$ of Strontium 90 (Sr-90) remaining at time t (in years) satisfies the differential equation $\dfrac{dQ}{dt} = -0.0231Q$. Solve to find $Q(t)$ if the initial amount of Sr-90 is 100mg. Find the half-life of Sr-90.

5. Answers to Sample Problems

(a) Show that $y = 5e^{-2t}$ is a solution to $\dfrac{dy}{dt} = -2y$.

$$\frac{dy}{dt} = 5(-2)e^{-2t} = -2y.$$

(b) Show that $y = Ae^{-kt}$ is a solution to $\dfrac{dy}{dt} = -ky$.

$$\frac{dy}{dt} = A(-k)e^{-kt} = -ky.$$

(c) Show that $y = 3x^2$ is a solution to $\dfrac{dy}{dx} = \dfrac{2y}{x}$.

$$\frac{dy}{dx} = 6x = \frac{6x^2}{x} = \frac{2y}{x}.$$

(d) Show that $y = Ax^3$ is a solution to $\dfrac{dy}{dx} = \dfrac{3y}{x}$.

$$\frac{dy}{dx} = 3Ax^2 = \frac{3Ax^3}{x} = \frac{3y}{x}.$$

(e) Solve $\dfrac{dy}{dx} = \cos x$. $y = \sin x + C$, where C can be any constant.

(f) Suppose that a population of bacteria grows at a rate proportional to its population, and assume that the constant of proportionality is 0.5hr^{-1}. Write down a differential equation stating this assumption. Solve it, assuming that the initial population is 4000 bacteria. Find the doubling time for this population.

The differential equation is $\frac{dP}{dt} = \frac{1}{2}P$. The solution is $P = 4000e^{t/2}$. To find the doubling time, we need to find the time when the population is 8000.

$$8000 = 4000e^{t/2} \Rightarrow 2 = e^{t/2} \Rightarrow \ln 2 = \frac{t}{2},$$

which means that the doubling time is $2\ln 2 \approx 1.4$ hours.

(g) The quantity $Q(t)$ of Strontium 90 (Sr-90) remaining at time t (in years) satisfies the differential equation $\frac{dQ}{dt} = -0.0231Q$. Solve to find $Q(t)$ if the initial amount of Sr-90 is 100mg. Find the half-life of Sr-90.

Solving the differential equation, we get $Q(t) = 100e^{-0.0231t}$. The half-life will be the time when there are 50mg remaining.

$$50 = 100e^{-0.0231t} \Rightarrow \frac{1}{2} = e^{-0.0231t} \Rightarrow \ln\frac{1}{2} = -0.0231t,$$

which means that the half-life of Sr-90 is $\frac{\ln 0.5}{-0.0231}$ years. Notice that this quantity is positive because $\ln 0.5$ is a negative number. In fact, using a calculator, we obtain a half life of 30 years.

5.4 Integrals and Applications

a. Derive definite integrals of standard algebraic functions using the formal definition of integral

1. What is the definition of the definite integral?

   The mathematical definition is below. We will see how to use it here, and then investigate what it means in later sections. The definite integral of f from $x = a$ to $x = b$ is:

$$\int_a^b f(x)\ dx = \lim_{n \to \infty} \left[\sum_{i=0}^{n-1} f(a + i\Delta x)\Delta x \right] \quad \text{OR} \quad \lim_{n \to \infty} \left[\sum_{i=1}^{n} f(a + i\Delta x)\Delta x \right],$$

   where $\Delta x = \dfrac{b-a}{n}$. The first comes from the "left-hand sums," while the second comes from the "right-hand sums."

2. How can you evaluate a definite integral using the definition?

   We will integrate $f(x) = x$ from $x = 2$ to $x = 5$ using this definition. First we write down $\Delta x = \dfrac{5-2}{n} = \dfrac{3}{n}$. Then we apply the formula:

$$
\begin{aligned}
\int_2^5 x\ dx &= \lim_{n \to \infty} \left[\sum_{i=1}^{n} f(2 + i\Delta x)\Delta x \right] = \lim_{n \to \infty} \left[\sum_{i=1}^{n} \left(2 + \frac{3i}{n} \right) \frac{3}{n} \right] = \\
&= \lim_{n \to \infty} \left[\sum_{i=1}^{n} \left(\frac{6}{n} + \frac{9i}{n^2} \right) \right] = \lim_{n \to \infty} \left[\sum_{i=1}^{n} \frac{6}{n} + \sum_{i=1}^{n} \frac{9i}{n^2} \right] = \\
&= \lim_{n \to \infty} \left[\frac{6}{n} \sum_{i=1}^{n} 1 + \frac{9}{n^2} \sum_{i=1}^{n} i \right] = \lim_{n \to \infty} \left[\frac{6}{n}(n) + \frac{9}{n^2} \left(\frac{n(n+1)}{2} \right) \right] = \\
&= \lim_{n \to \infty} \left[6 + \frac{9}{2} + \frac{9}{2n} \right] = \frac{21}{2} = 10.5.
\end{aligned}
$$

3. What other information do we need to know in order to use the definition of the integral?

   As you could tell from the example, we had to know the "closed form" of certain summations. Some helpful ones are listed below:

$$\sum_{i=1}^{n} 1 = n; \quad \sum_{i=1}^{n} i = \frac{n(n+1)}{2}; \quad \sum_{i=1}^{n} i^2 = \frac{n(n+1)(2n+1)}{6}.$$

   We also had to recall how the distributive property relates to summations: if k doesn't depend on i, then $\sum_{i=1}^{n} ka_i = k \sum_{i=1}^{n} a_i$.

4. Sample Problems

(a) Calculate $\int_2^7 (x-4)\,dx$ using the definition of the definite integral.

(b) Calculate $\int_0^3 x^2\,dx$ using the definition of the definite integral.

5. Answers to Sample Problems

(a) Calculate $\int_2^7 (x-4)\,dx$ using the definition of the definite integral.

$$
\begin{aligned}
\int_2^7 (x-4)\,dx &= \lim_{n\to\infty}\left[\sum_{i=1}^n (2+i\Delta x - 4)\Delta x\right] = \lim_{n\to\infty}\left[\sum_{i=1}^n \left(-2+\frac{5i}{n}\right)\frac{5}{n}\right] \\
&= \lim_{n\to\infty}\left[\sum_{i=1}^n \left(\frac{-10}{n}+\frac{25i}{n^2}\right)\right] = \lim_{n\to\infty}\left[\sum_{i=1}^n \frac{-10}{n}+\sum_{i=1}^n \frac{25i}{n^2}\right] \\
&= \lim_{n\to\infty}\left[\frac{-10}{n}(n)+\frac{25}{n^2}\sum_{i=1}^n i\right] = \lim_{n\to\infty}\left[-10+\frac{25}{n^2}\frac{n(n+1)}{2}\right] \\
&= \lim_{n\to\infty}\left[-10+\frac{25}{2}\frac{n(n+1)}{n^2}\right] = -10+\frac{25}{2} = \frac{5}{2}.
\end{aligned}
$$

(b) Calculate $\int_0^3 x^2\,dx$ using the definition of the definite integral.

$$
\begin{aligned}
\int_0^3 x^2\,dx &= \lim_{n\to\infty}\left[\sum_{i=1}^n (0+i\Delta x)^2\Delta x\right] = \lim_{n\to\infty}\left[\sum_{i=1}^n \left(\frac{3i}{n}\right)^2\frac{3}{n}\right] \\
&= \lim_{n\to\infty}\frac{27}{n^3}\sum_{i=1}^n i^2 = \lim_{n\to\infty}\frac{27}{n^3}\left(\frac{n(n+1)(2n+1)}{6}\right) \\
&= \frac{27}{6}\lim_{n\to\infty}\left(\frac{n(n+1)(2n+1)}{n^3}\right) = \frac{27}{6}(2) = 9.
\end{aligned}
$$

b. Interpret the concept of a definite integral geometrically, numerically, and analytically (e.g., limit of Riemann sums)

1. How is the concept of the definite integral related to the definition?

   The integral is most commonly thought of as "area under the curve." There are several ways to approximate the area between a graph of $y = f(x)$ and the x-axis, but the two easiest ones to use are the left-hand sums and right-hand sums. In each method, rectangles are used to estimate the area between $y = f(x)$ and the x-axis (top and bottom boundaries), and between $x = a$ and $x = b$ (left and right boundaries). Both methods begin by dividing the interval $[a, b]$ into n equal subdivisions, each of width Δx, which is why $\Delta x = \dfrac{b-a}{n}$.

   The left-hand sums (LHS) form rectangles on each subinterval, with the height of the rectangle being determined by the value of f at the LEFT endpoint of the subinterval. (So, the first rectangle has height $f(a)$, the second $f(a+\Delta x)$, the third $f(a+2\Delta x)$, etc.)

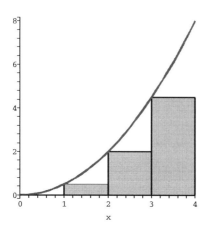 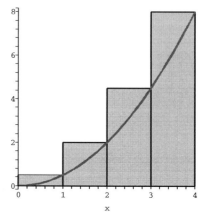

Example: LHS and RHS approximations to $\int_0^4 \dfrac{x^2}{2}\, dx$ **with** $n = 4$

The right-hand sums (RHS) use rectangles whose heights are determined by the value of the function at the RIGHT endpoint of each subinterval. (So, the first rectangle has height $f(a + \Delta x)$, the second $f(a + 2\Delta x)$, the third $f(a + 3\Delta x)$, etc.) Thus, the area obtained by each method is slightly different:

$$\text{LHS} \;=\; f(a)\Delta x + f(a+\Delta x)\Delta x + \ldots + f(a+(n-1)\Delta x)\Delta x = \sum_{i=0}^{n-1} f(a+i\Delta x)\Delta x$$

$$\text{RHS} \;=\; f(a+\Delta x)\Delta x + f(a+2\Delta x)\Delta x + \ldots + f(a+n\Delta x)\Delta x = \sum_{i=1}^{n} f(a+i\Delta x)\Delta x$$

However, for suitably "nice" (*integrable*) functions, these two approximations for area approach the same value in the limit as n, the number of subdivisions, increases to infinity. Therefore, the definite integral is defined as the limit of these summations as n approaches infinity.

2. What does the definite integral mean geometrically? ... numerically? ... analytically?

   Geometrically, the definite integral refers to the area under the curve. Numerically speaking, one can approximate this area in a variety of ways, usually by using LHS or RHS with a small number of subdivisions. This method works even if you only have a table of function values. (See Sample Problems.) Analytically, one can use the Fundamental Theorem of Calculus to evaluate definite integrals. (See next section.)

3. What are some properties of integrals?

   Let a, b, and k be constants.

   - $\displaystyle \int_a^b k f(x)\, dx = k \int_a^b f(x)\, dx$

   - $\displaystyle \int_a^b f(x)\, dx = - \int_b^a f(x)\, dx$

- $$\int_a^b f(x)\ dx = \int_a^c f(x)\ dx + \int_c^b f(x)\ dx$$

All of these properties follow from the definition, and can be interpreted in terms of area under the curve.

4. What is a Riemann sum? (pronounced: REE-mahn, not RYE-mahn)

Bernhard Riemann (1826-1866) contributed to the subject of Analysis (the branch of mathematics which includes calculus) when he defined the definite integral as a limit of summations. Today, a sum which approximates the area under a curve is called a Riemann sum. Thus, both the summations given in the above definition of the definite integral are Riemann sums. Riemann was actually more general in his definition, allowing for subintervals which were not necessarily of the same length, and using any point in the subinterval to determine the rectangle height. This gives a more complicated formula, but one which still converges to the same value.

The Riemann integral is thus

$$\int_a^b f(x)\ dx = \lim_{n\to\infty} \sum_{i=1}^n f(c_i)(x_i - x_{i-1}),$$

where $a = x_0 < x_1 < \ldots < x_{n-1} < x_n = b$ and $x_{i-1} \le c_i \le x_i$.

5. Sample Problems

   (a) Evaluate $\int_2^5 x\ dx$ using area under the curve.

   (b) Evaluate $\int_0^3 \sqrt{9 - x^2}\ dx$ exactly.

   (c) Using the following table, estimate $\int_0^{20} f(x)\ dx$ using left-hand sums, and right-hand sums, and then averaging the two estimates.

x	0	5	10	15	20
$f(x)$	1	3	4	6	11

   (d) If $\int_2^5 f(x)\ dx = 7$ and $\int_2^9 f(x)\ dx = 5$, then find $\int_5^9 f(x)\ dx$.

   (e) Explain how $\int_a^b f\ dx = -\int_b^a f\ dx$ follows from the definition of the definite integral.

6. Answers to Sample Problems

   (a) Evaluate $\int_2^5 x\ dx$ using area under the curve. The trapezoid has area $\frac{(2+5)(3)}{2} = \frac{21}{2}$.

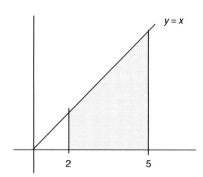

(b) Evaluate $\int_0^3 \sqrt{9-x^2}\, dx$ exactly. Notice that if $y = \sqrt{9-x^2}$, then $y^2 = 9 - x^2$, or $x^2 + y^2 = 9$, which is the graph of a circle of radius 3. The quarter circle described has area $\frac{1}{4}\pi(3)^2 = \frac{9\pi}{4}$.

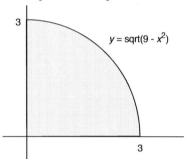

(c) Using the following table, estimate $\int_0^{20} f(x)\, dx$ using left-hand sums, and right-hand sums, and then averaging the two estimates.

x	0	5	10	15	20
$f(x)$	1	3	4	6	11

Using left hand sums, we have four boxes, each of width 5, with heights 1, 3, 4, and 6. So the area is

$$5(1) + 5(3) + 5(4) + 5(6) = 5(1 + 3 + 4 + 6) = 5(14) = 70.$$

Similarly, the right hand sums give an area of $5(3 + 4 + 6 + 11) = 5(24) = 120$. The average of these two estimates is 95.

(d) If $\int_2^5 f(x)\, dx = 7$ and $\int_2^9 f(x)\, dx = 5$, then find $\int_5^9 f(x)\, dx$.

One property of definite integrals implies that

$$\int_2^5 f(x)\, dx + \int_5^9 f(x)\, dx = \int_2^9 f(x)\, dx.$$

So, $7 + \int_5^9 f(x)\, dx = 5$, which means $\int_5^9 f(x)\, dx = -2$.

(e) Explain how $\int_a^b f\, dx = -\int_b^a f\, dx$ follows from the definition of the definite integral.

Recall the definition of the definite integral:

$$\int_a^b f(x)\ dx = \lim_{n\to\infty}\left[\sum_{i=0}^{n-1} f(a+i\Delta x)\Delta x\right] \quad \text{OR} \quad \lim_{n\to\infty}\left[\sum_{i=1}^{n} f(a+i\Delta x)\Delta x\right],$$

where $\Delta x = \dfrac{b-a}{n}$. So, if we switch a and b, we wind up changing the sign of Δx. This introduces a negative sign in every term of the sum. (It also means that we sum the boxes from right to left, but that alone would not change the sign of the answer.) Therefore, $\displaystyle\int_a^b f\ dx = -\int_b^a f\ dx$.

c. Prove the fundamental theorem of calculus, and use it to interpret definite integrals as antiderivatives

1. What does the Fundamental Theorem of Calculus (FTOC) say?

   In the last section, we studied derivatives, and this section, we are studying integrals. These are the two main concepts of Calculus. They arise in different ways (slopes of tangent lines vs. areas under curves), yet they are intimately related through the most important theorem of calculus:

   Part 1: If f is continuous on $[a,b]$ then $F(x) := \displaystyle\int_a^x f(t)\ dt$ is continuous on $[a,b]$, differentiable on (a,b), and $F'(x) = f(x)$.

   Part 2: If f is continuous on $[a,b]$ and if F is any antiderivative of f (that is, $F' = f$), then
   $$\int_a^b f(t)\ dt = F(b) - F(a).$$

2. How do you prove the FTOC?

   We will prove Part 1 by using the definition of the derivative and our ideas about area. The main result of Part 1 is that the derivative of F is f. So let's start with the definition of the derivative of F and see where we go.

   $$F'(x) = \lim_{h\to 0}\frac{F(x+h) - F(x)}{h} = \lim_{h\to 0}\frac{\int_a^{x+h} f(t)\ dt - \int_a^x f(t)\ dt}{h}$$
   $$= \lim_{h\to 0}\frac{1}{h}\left(\int_x^{x+h} f(t)\ dt\right)$$

   Let's think about what's happening here. Since f is continuous, we know that as $h \to 0$, $f(x+h) \to f(x)$, which means that this integral can be approximated by a rectangle of height $f(x)$ and width h. So,

   $$\lim_{h\to 0}\frac{1}{h}\left(\int_x^{x+h} f(t)\ dt\right) = \lim_{h\to 0}\frac{1}{h}[f(x)h] = f(x).$$

   So, $F'(x) = f(x)$, which is what we set out to prove. [Note: we can be more precise. In fact, because f is continuous, there is some value c between x and $x+h$ that makes

$\int_x^{x+h} f(t)\ dt = f(c)h$. Then as $h \to 0$, $f(c) \to f(x)$. But the hand-wavy argument has the same spirit.] $\square$

We will prove Part 2 using Part 1. Since f is continuous, we know from Part 1 that the function $G(x) = \int_a^x f(t)\ dt$ is an antiderivative of f. So, $(F-G)' = F' - G' = f - f = 0$, which means that $F - G$ must be a constant. So, $F(x) = G(x) + C$. Therefore,

$$\begin{aligned} F(b) - F(a) &= [G(b) + C] - [G(a) + C] = G(b) - G(a) = \\ &= \int_a^b f(t)\ dt - \int_a^a f(t)\ dt = \int_a^b f(t)\ dt, \end{aligned}$$

which is what we set out to prove. $\square$

3. How does the FTOC allow you to interpret definite integrals as antiderivatives?

   Part 2 is the way that most definite integrals are evaluated. All you have to do is find any antiderivative of the integrand and then evaluate at b and at a and take the difference. As an example, let us consider the definite integral we did at the beginning: $\int_2^5 x\ dx$. Using FTOC Part 2, we need to find an antiderivative of x. It's not too hard to see that $F(x) = \dfrac{x^2}{2}$ works, because $F'(x) = x$. Therefore

$$\int_2^5 x\ dx = \left.\frac{x^2}{2}\right|_2^5 = \frac{5^2}{2} - \frac{2^2}{2} = \frac{21}{2} = 10.5.$$

   This method is much faster than using the definition to evaluate definite integrals.

4. Sample Problems

   (a) Calculate the following definite integrals.

   i. $\displaystyle\int_0^4 x^2\ dx$

   ii. $\displaystyle\int_0^\pi \sin x\ dx$

   iii. $\displaystyle\int_0^\pi \cos x\ dx$ [Why?]

   iv. $\displaystyle\int_0^1 x^n\ dx$

   v. $\displaystyle\int_0^3 e^x\ dx$

   vi. $\displaystyle\int_3^8 \frac{7}{x^2}\ dx$

   vii. $\displaystyle\int_3^5 (3x^2 + 2x - 1)\ dx$

   viii. $\displaystyle\int_{-2}^2 (x^4 - 5x^2 + 4)\ dx$

(b) Differentiate the following functions.

    i. $F(x) = \int_2^x (4t^3 - t^2 + t + 1) \, dt$

    ii. $F(x) = \int_x^{10} (e^t + 24 \sin t - \ln t) \, dt$

    iii. $F(x) = \int_2^4 (t^3 - t) \, dt$

    iv. $F(x) = \int_x^{x+5} (e^{3t} + \sqrt{7t - 2}) \, dt$

(c) Calculate the following definite integrals.

    i. $\int_0^1 e^{5x} \, dx$

    ii. $\int_0^{\pi/3} \sin 3x \, dx$

    iii. $\int_2^5 \dfrac{x}{x^2 + 1} \, dx$

5. Answers to Sample Problems

(a) Calculate the following definite integrals.

    i. $\int_0^4 x^2 \, dx = \dfrac{x^3}{3}\Big|_0^4 = \dfrac{64}{3}$

    ii. $\int_0^\pi \sin x \, dx = (-\cos x)\big|_0^\pi = 2$

    iii. $\int_0^\pi \cos x \, dx = 0$, because if you look at the graph, the area above the x-axis is equal to the area below the x-axis.

    iv. $\int_0^1 x^n \, dx = \dfrac{x^{n+1}}{n+1}\Big|_0^1 = \dfrac{1}{n+1}$

    v. $\int_0^3 e^x \, dx = e^x\big|_0^3 = e^3 - 1$

    vi. $\int_3^8 \dfrac{7}{x^2} \, dx = -\dfrac{7}{x}\Big|_3^8 = -\dfrac{7}{8} + \dfrac{7}{3} = \dfrac{35}{24}$

    vii. $\int_3^5 (3x^2 + 2x - 1) \, dx = (x^3 + x^2 - x)\big|_3^5 = 112$

    viii. $\int_{-2}^2 (x^4 - 5x^2 + 4) \, dx = \left(\dfrac{x^5}{5} - \dfrac{5x^3}{3} + 4x\right)\Big|_{-2}^2 = \dfrac{32}{15}$

(b) Differentiate the following functions.

    i. $F(x) = \int_2^x (4t^3 - t^2 + t + 1) \, dt$; $F'(x) = 4x^3 - x^2 + x + 1$.

ii. $F(x) = \int_x^{10} (e^t + 24\sin t - \ln t)\, dt$; $F'(x) = -e^x - 24\sin x + \ln x$.

iii. $F(x) = \int_2^4 (t^3 - t)\, dt$; $F'(x) = 0$ (because $F(x)$ is a constant).

iv. $F(x) = \int_x^{x+5} (e^{3t} + \sqrt{7t - 2})\, dt$

If we separate into two integrals (at $x = 0$, say), we have

$$F(x) = \int_x^0 (e^{3t} + \sqrt{7t - 2})\, dt + \int_0^{x+5} (e^{3t} + \sqrt{7t - 2})\, dt.$$

Therefore,

$$\begin{aligned} F'(x) &= -(e^{3x} + \sqrt{7x - 2}) + e^{3(x+5)} + \sqrt{7(x+5)} - 2 \\ &= e^{3x+15} - e^{3x} + \sqrt{7x + 33} - \sqrt{7x - 2}. \end{aligned}$$

(c) Calculate the following definite integrals.

i. $\int_0^1 e^{5x}\, dx = \left. \frac{1}{5} e^{5x} \right|_0^1 = \frac{1}{5} e^5 - \frac{1}{5}$

ii. $\int_0^{\pi/3} \sin 3x\, dx = \left. -\frac{1}{3} \cos 3x \right|_0^{\pi/3} = \frac{1}{3} + \frac{1}{3} = \frac{2}{3}$

iii. $\int_2^5 \frac{x}{x^2 + 1}\, dx = \left. \frac{1}{2} \ln(x^2 + 1) \right|_2^5 = \frac{1}{2} \ln(26) - \frac{1}{2} \ln(5) = \frac{1}{2} \ln\left(\frac{26}{5} \right)$

If it is difficult to guess the antiderivative in these problems, you can use the method of Substitution. In the third problem, we can let $u = x^2 + 1$. Everything else follows from this choice of u. Then $\frac{du}{dx} = 2x$, which means that $x\, dx = \frac{du}{2}$. Next, the limits need to be changed. When $x = 2$, $u = 5$, and when $x = 5$, $u = 26$. Thus,

$$\int_2^5 \frac{x\, dx}{x^2 + 1} = \int_5^{26} \frac{1}{u} \frac{du}{2} = \frac{1}{2} \int_5^{26} \frac{1}{u}\, du = \left. \frac{1}{2} \ln(u) \right|_5^{26} = \frac{1}{2} \ln(26) - \frac{1}{2} \ln(5).$$

d. Apply the concept of integrals to compute the length of curves and the areas and volumes of geometric figures

1. How is the concept of the integral applied to other problems?

   The main idea of the definite integral is that it is a way to add up a lot of tiny contributions to a quantity, giving the total amount of that quantity, even if the individual contributions are not constant over time or across space. For instance, physicists use integration to calculate work done, distance traveled, etc.

2. How does integration apply to rectilinear motion?

   Since velocity is the derivative of displacement (i.e., position), then one can determine how far an object has traveled if one integrates its velocity function. For example, if a particle has a velocity of $4t$ m/s from $t = 0$ to $t = 3$ seconds, then the object travels

$$\int_0^3 4t\, dt = \left. 2t^2 \right|_0^3 = 18 \text{ meters.}$$

3. How can you use the definite integral to measure area between two curves?

By breaking the region into rectangles, one can deduce that the area between the graphs of $f(x)$ and $g(x)$, between $x = a$ and $x = b$ is $\int_a^b [f(x) - g(x)]dx$, assuming $f(x) > g(x)$. For example, the area between $y = \sin x$ and $y = \cos x$ from $x = \pi/4$ to $x = 5\pi/4$ is

$$\int_{\pi/4}^{5\pi/4} (\sin x - \cos x)dx = [-\cos x - \sin x]\Big|_{\pi/4}^{5\pi/4} = +\frac{\sqrt{2}}{2} + \frac{\sqrt{2}}{2} + \frac{\sqrt{2}}{2} + \frac{\sqrt{2}}{2} = 2\sqrt{2}.$$

4. How can you use the definite integral to measure the length of a function curve (arc length)?

By breaking a curve into small straight lines, one can deduce that the arc length of $y = f(x)$ above the interval $[a, b]$ is $\int_a^b \sqrt{1 + (f'(x))^2}\, dx$. The problem is that there are very few functions for which the arc length works out nicely. The length of $y = \frac{2}{3}x^{3/2}$ from $x = 0$ to $x = 2$ can be worked out. Note that $f'(x) = x^{1/2}$.

$$L = \int_0^2 \sqrt{1 + x}\, dx = \int_1^3 u^{1/2}\, du = \frac{2}{3}u^{3/2}\Big|_1^3 = \frac{2}{3}[3^{3/2} - 1] = 2\sqrt{3} - \frac{2}{3},$$

where we used the substitution method of integration (with $u = 1+x$) to evaluate the integral.

5. How can you use the definite integral to measure the surface area of a solid of revolution?

The formula for surface area is similar to that of arc length, only it takes into account the radius of revolution (which is just $y = f(x)$ when the axis of revolution is the x-axis). The surface area of the solid formed by rotating $f(x)$ around the x-axis is $\int_a^b 2\pi f(x)\sqrt{1 + (f'(x))^2}\, dx$. Like arc length, surface area integrals rarely work out nicely.

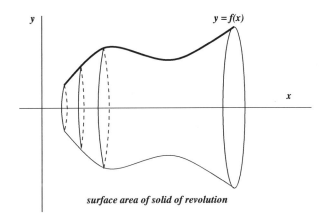

surface area of solid of revolution

As an example, we can rotate $y = \frac{1}{3}x^3$ from $x = 1$ to $x = 4$ around the x-axis and find the surface area of the solid generated. Notice that $f'(x) = x^2$ here, and again, we need substitution.

$$\begin{aligned} SA &= \int_1^4 2\pi \left(\frac{x^3}{3}\right)\sqrt{1 + x^4}\, dx = \frac{2\pi}{12}\int_1^4 4x^3\sqrt{1 + x^4}\, dx \\ &= \frac{\pi}{6}\left(\frac{2}{3}(1 + x^4)^{3/2}\right)\Big|_1^4 = \frac{\pi}{9}(257^{3/2} - 2^{3/2}). \end{aligned}$$

6. How can you use the definite integral to measure the volume of a solid of revolution?

   To measure the volume of a solid of revolution, one can think of the solid as being divided into small slices (usually disks or washers). Then one can find the area of each slice. By integrating the area over all possible slices, one obtains the volume. For example, if $y = f(x) > 0$ is rotated around the x-axis, the volume generated between a and b is $\displaystyle\int_a^b \pi(f(x))^2\ dx$.

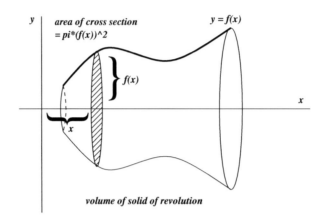

   For example, rotating the curve $y = \sqrt{x}$ around the x-axis between $x = 4$ and $x = 9$ gives a volume of:
   $$V = \int_4^9 \pi(\sqrt{x})^2 dx = \int_4^9 \pi x\ dx = \left.\frac{\pi x^2}{2}\right|_4^9 = \frac{65\pi}{2}.$$

7. How can you use the definite integral to measure the volume of a solid that has a consistent cross-sectional shape?

   Suppose that the cross-sections have an area function $A(x)$. Then the volume of the solid (from $x = a$ to $x = b$) is $\displaystyle\int_a^b A(x)\ dx$. For example, if we want to find the volume of a pyramid that is 5 feet tall and has a square base of side length 5 feet, then we can think of the pyramid as being composed of square slices that are parallel to the base. Indeed, the slice that is x feet above the ground has a side length of $5 - x$ feet. So its area is $(5 - x)^2 = 25 - 10x + x^2$. Integrating over all values of x, we get the volume:

   $$\begin{aligned} V &= \int_0^5 (25 - 10x + x^2)dx \\ &= \left[25x - 5x^2 + \frac{x^3}{3}\right]\Big|_0^5 \\ &= 125 - 125 + \frac{125}{3} = \frac{125}{3}\text{ cubic feet.} \end{aligned}$$

8. Sample Problems

   (a) Find the area between x^2 and x^3, from $x = 0$ to $x = 1$.

(b) Find the arc length of $y = 2x$ from $x = 0$ to $x = 4$ using integration. Then compare your answer to the Pythagorean Theorem.

(c) The following graph represents the velocity of a helicopter. Estimate the distance traveled by the helicopter in the first 20 minutes. ...in the first 60 minutes.

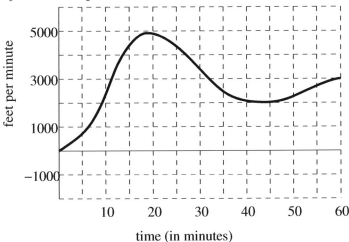

(d) Find the surface area of the solid generated by rotating $y = \frac{1}{3}x$ around the x-axis, from $x = 0$ to $x = 7$. What does this solid look like?

(e) Find the volume generated by rotating $y = \sqrt{\sin x}$ from 0 to π around the x-axis.

(f) Find the volume generated by rotating $y = 4 - x^2$ from -2 to 2 around the x-axis.

(g) Find the volume of the solid whose base is the unit circle, but whose cross-sections perpendicular to the x-axis are squares.

(h) Find the area between x^n and x^m ($n > m > 0$), from $x = 0$ to $x = 1$.

(i) Find the surface area of the solid generated by rotating $y = mx$ around the x-axis, from $x = 0$ to $x = H$. From this, deduce the formula for the lateral surface area of a cone of height H and radius R.

(j) Using the same equations as the previous problem, find the volume of the cone.

9. Answers to Sample Problems

(a) Find the area between x^2 and x^3, from $x = 0$ to $x = 1$. $\displaystyle\int_0^1 (x^2 - x^3)\, dx = \frac{1}{12}$

(b) Find the arc length of $y = 2x$ from $x = 0$ to $x = 4$ using integration. Then compare your answer to the Pythagorean Theorem. $4\sqrt{5}$

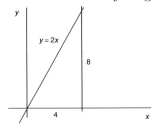

$$\int_0^4 \sqrt{1+4}\, dx = 4\sqrt{5} = \sqrt{80} = \sqrt{4^2 + 8^2}$$

(c) The following graph represents the velocity of a helicopter. Estimate the distance traveled by the helicopter in the first 20 minutes. ... in the first 60 minutes.

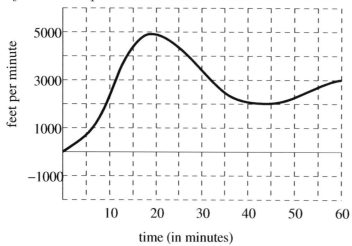

Answers may vary. The area between 0 and 20 is about 10 boxes, which means that the helicopter travels approximately $(10)(5)(1000) = 50{,}000$ feet in the first 20 minutes. In the first 60 minutes, the helicopter travels approximately $(23)(5)(1000) = 115{,}000$ feet.

(d) Find the surface area of the solid generated by rotating $y = \frac{1}{3}x$ around the x-axis, from $x = 0$ to $x = 7$. What does this solid look like? This solid is a cone. The surface area is

$$\int_0^7 2\pi \left(\frac{x}{3}\right) \sqrt{1 + \left(\frac{1}{3}\right)^2}\ dx = \frac{2\pi\sqrt{10}}{9} \int_0^7 x\ dx = \frac{49\pi\sqrt{10}}{9}.$$

(e) Find the volume generated by rotating $y = \sqrt{\sin x}$ from 0 to π around the x-axis.

$$\int_0^\pi \pi \sin x\ dx = -\pi \cos x \big|_0^\pi = 2\pi$$

(f) Find the volume generated by rotating $y = 4 - x^2$ from -2 to 2 around the x-axis.

$$\int_{-2}^2 \pi (4 - x^2)^2\ dx = \pi \int_{-2}^2 (16 - 8x^2 + x^4)\ dx = \frac{512\pi}{15}$$

(g) Find the volume of the solid whose base is the unit circle, but whose cross-sections perpendicular to the x-axis are squares. A picture of this solid is given below.

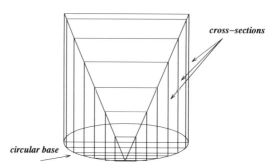

The circular boundary is $y = \pm\sqrt{1 - x^2}$. So the side length of the square at x-coordinate x is $2\sqrt{1 - x^2}$. The volume is thus:

$$\int_{-1}^{1} \left(2\sqrt{1 - x^2}\right)^2 \, dx = \int_{-1}^{1} (4 - 4x^2) \, dx = \left(4x - \frac{4x^3}{3}\right)\Big|_{-1}^{1} = \frac{16}{3}$$

(h) Find the area between x^n and x^m $(n > m > 0)$, from $x = 0$ to $x = 1$.

$$\int_{0}^{1} (x^m - x^n) \, dx = \left(\frac{x^{m+1}}{m+1} - \frac{x^{n+1}}{n+1}\right)\Big|_{0}^{1} = \frac{1}{m+1} - \frac{1}{n+1} = \frac{n - m}{(m+1)(n+1)}$$

(i) Find the surface area of the solid generated by rotating $y = mx$ around the x-axis, from $x = 0$ to $x = H$. From this, deduce the formula for the lateral surface area of a cone of height H and radius R.

$$\int_{0}^{H} 2\pi m x \sqrt{1 + m^2} \, dx = 2\pi m \sqrt{1 + m^2} \int_{0}^{H} x \, dx = \pi m H^2 \sqrt{1 + m^2}$$

Notice that the slope m is equal to $\frac{R}{H}$. So the surface area formula simplifies to

$$\pi m H^2 \sqrt{1 + m^2} = \pi \left(\frac{R}{H}\right) H^2 \sqrt{1 + \left(\frac{R}{H}\right)^2} = \pi R \sqrt{H^2 + R^2} = \pi R \ell,$$

where ℓ is the *slant height* of the cone.

(j) Using the same equations as the previous problem, find the volume of the cone.

$$\int_{0}^{H} \pi (mx)^2 \, dx = \pi m^2 \left(\frac{x^3}{3}\right)\Big|_{0}^{H} = \frac{\pi m^2 H^3}{3} = \frac{1}{3}\pi R^2 H,$$

where again we used the fact that $m = \frac{R}{H}$.

5.5 Sequences and Series

a. Derive and apply the formulas for the sums of finite arithmetic series and finite and infinite geometric series (e.g., express repeating decimals as a rational number)

1. What is the difference between an "arithmetic" sequence and a "geometric" sequence?

   A sequence is "arithmetic" if there is a *common difference* between successive terms. For example, the sequence 1, 4, 7, 10, 13, 16, ... is arithmetic. The formula for the n-th term of an arithmetic sequence is linear: $a_n = a_1 + (n-1)d$, where d is the common difference and a_1 is the first term.

   A sequence is "geometric" if there is a *common ratio* between successive terms. For example, the sequence $\frac{1}{2}$, 1, 2, 4, 8, ... is geometric. The formula for the n-th term of a geometric sequence is exponential: $a_n = a_1 r^{n-1}$, where r is the common ratio and a_1 is the first term.

2. How do you derive a formula for the sum of a finite arithmetic sequence?

   Let's do an example first. Suppose we want to find: $1 + 4 + 7 + 10 + 13 + 16$ using a shortcut.

$$\begin{array}{ccccccc} 1 & +4 & +7 & +10 & +13 & +16 & = & S \\ +16 & +13 & +10 & +7 & +4 & +1 & = & S \\ \hline 17 & +17 & +17 & +17 & +17 & +17 & = & 2S \end{array}$$

   And so $S = \dfrac{(17)(6)}{2} = 51$. It's not hard to see that

$$S_n = a_1 + a_2 + \ldots + a_n = \frac{n}{2}(a_1 + a_n) \quad \text{or} \quad S = \frac{n}{2}(2a_1 + (n-1)d).$$

3. How do you derive the formula for the sum of a finite geometric sequence?

   Let's do another example first. Suppose we want to add up $\frac{1}{2} + 1 + 2 + 4 + 8$ using a shortcut.

$$\begin{array}{ccccccc} \frac{1}{2} & +1 & +2 & +4 & +8 & = & S \\ -(1 & +2 & +4 & +8 & +16 & = & 2S) \\ \hline \frac{1}{2} & +0 & +0 & +0 & -16 & = & -S \end{array}$$

   And so $S = \dfrac{\frac{1}{2} - 16}{-1} = \dfrac{31}{2}$. Repeating this in general gives

$$S_n = a_1 + a_1 r + \ldots + a_1 r^{n-1} = \frac{a_1 - a_1 r^n}{1 - r}.$$

4. When can you extend the formula for the sum of a finite geometric sequence to an infinite geometric sequence? What do you obtain?

   If $|r| < 1$, then the terms of the geometric series approach 0 as $n \to \infty$. So, if we calculate $S = \lim_{n \to \infty} S_n$, we get $S = \dfrac{a_1}{1-r}$. If $|r| \geq 1$, then the infinite geometric series does not converge.

5. How can you represent a repeating decimal as a rational number?

   Every repeating decimal is really a geometric series in disguise. For example,

   $$0.\overline{15} = \frac{15}{100} + \frac{15}{10,000} + \frac{15}{1,000,000} + \ldots = \frac{\frac{15}{100}}{1 - \frac{1}{100}} = \frac{15}{99} = \frac{5}{33}.$$

6. Sample Problems

   (a) Find the sum of the first 100 positive integers. [Gauss did this in second grade, according to math legend.]

   (b) Find the sum of the first 100 positive even integers.

   (c) Find the sum of the following series.

      i. $36 + 12 + 4 + \frac{4}{3} + \frac{4}{9} + \frac{4}{27}$

      ii. $36 + 12 + 4 + \frac{4}{3} + \frac{4}{9} + \frac{4}{27} + \ldots$

      iii. $\frac{1}{2} + \frac{1}{4} + \frac{1}{8} + \frac{1}{16} + \ldots$

      iv. $\frac{2}{3} + \frac{4}{9} + \frac{8}{27} + \frac{16}{81} + \ldots$

      v. $1 - 1 + 1 - 1 + \ldots + (-1)^n$

      vi. $1 + 1.1 + 1.21 + 1.331 + 1.4641 + \ldots + (1.1)^{10}$

   (d) Fill in the details to derive the arithmetic sum formula $S_n = \frac{n}{2}(a_1 + a_n)$.

   (e) Fill in the details to derive the geometric sum formula $S_n = \frac{a_1 - a_1 r^n}{1 - r}$.

   (f) Find rational values of the following.

      i. $0.\overline{4}$

      ii. $0.\overline{9}$

      iii. $0.\overline{123}$

      iv. $0.\overline{142857}$

7. Answers to Sample Problems

   (a) Find the sum of the first 100 positive integers. [Gauss did this in second grade, according to math legend.] $\frac{(1+100)(100)}{2} = 5050$.

   (b) Find the sum of the first 100 positive even integers.

   $$2 + 4 + \ldots + 200 = \frac{100}{2}(2 + 200) = 10{,}100$$

   (c) Find the sum of the following series.

      i. $36 + 12 + 4 + \frac{4}{3} + \frac{4}{9} + \frac{4}{27} = \frac{36 - \frac{4}{81}}{1 - \frac{1}{3}} = \frac{1456}{27}$

ii. $36 + 12 + 4 + \dfrac{4}{3} + \dfrac{4}{9} + \dfrac{4}{27} + \ldots = \dfrac{36}{1 - \frac{1}{3}} = 54$

iii. $\dfrac{1}{2} + \dfrac{1}{4} + \dfrac{1}{8} + \dfrac{1}{16} + \ldots = \dfrac{\frac{1}{2}}{1 - \frac{1}{2}} = 1$

iv. $\dfrac{2}{3} + \dfrac{4}{9} + \dfrac{8}{27} + \dfrac{16}{81} + \ldots = \dfrac{\frac{2}{3}}{1 - \frac{2}{3}} = 2$

v. $1 - 1 + 1 - 1 + \ldots + (-1)^n$. It depends. If n is even, then the sum is 1. If n is odd, then the sum is 0. Notice that this series starts at $n = 0$.

vi. $1 + 1.1 + 1.21 + 1.331 + 1.4641 + \ldots + (1.1)^{10} = \dfrac{1 - (1.1)^{11}}{1 - 1.1} = 10[(1.1)^{11} - 1] \approx 18.53$
(using a calculator)

(d) Fill in the details to derive the arithmetic sum formula $S_n = \dfrac{n}{2}(a_1 + a_n)$. First, notice that $a_1 + a_n = a_2 + a_{n-1}$ because the sequence is arithmetic. In other words:

$$a_2 + a_{n-1} = (a_1 + d) + a_{n-1} = a_1 + (d + a_{n-1}) = a_1 + a_n.$$

It's not hard to see that for all j, $a_j + a_{n+1-j} = a_1 + a_n$ for the same reason. So we have

$$
\begin{array}{ccccccc}
a_1 & +a_2 & +\ldots & +a_n & = & S \\
+a_n & +a_{n-1} & +\ldots & +a_1 & = & S \\
\hline
(a_1 + a_n) & +(a_1 + a_n) & +\ldots & +(a_1 + a_n) & = & 2S
\end{array}
$$

Therefore $S = \dfrac{n}{2}(a_1 + a_n)$.

(e) Fill in the details to derive the geometric sum formula $S_n = \dfrac{a_1 - a_1 r^n}{1 - r}$.

$$
\begin{array}{ccccccc}
a_1 & +a_1 r & +\ldots & +a_1 r^{n-1} & = & S_n \\
-(a_1 r & +a_1 r^2 & +\ldots & +a_1 r^n & = & rS_n) \\
\hline
a_1 & +0 & +\ldots & -a_1 r^n & = & (1-r)S_n
\end{array}
$$

Therefore, $S_n = \dfrac{a_1 - a_1 r^n}{1 - r}$.

(f) Find rational values of the following.

i. $0.\overline{4} = \dfrac{4}{9}$

ii. $0.\overline{9} = \dfrac{9}{9} = 1$

iii. $0.\overline{123} = \dfrac{123}{999} = \dfrac{41}{333}$

iv. $0.\overline{142857} = \dfrac{142{,}857}{999{,}999} = \dfrac{1}{7}$

b. Determine convergence of a given sequence or series using standard techniques (e.g., ratio, comparison, integral tests)

1. What does it mean for a sequence to converge?

    The sequence of terms a_n converges if $\lim\limits_{n\to\infty} a_n$ exists. For instance, the sequence $\frac{1}{2}, \frac{2}{3}, \frac{3}{4}, \frac{4}{5}, \ldots$ converges to 1, whereas the sequence $-1, 1, -1, 1, -1, 1, \ldots$ does not converge.

2. What does it mean for a series to converge?

    A series converges if and only if its "sequence of partial sums" converges. That means that the series $\sum\limits_{n=1}^{\infty} a_n$ converges if and only if the sequence

$$
\begin{aligned}
s_1 &= a_1 \\
s_2 &= a_1 + a_2 \\
s_3 &= a_1 + a_2 + a_3 \\
s_4 &= a_1 + a_2 + a_3 + a_4 \\
s_5 &= a_1 + a_2 + a_3 + a_4 + a_5
\end{aligned}
$$

etc.

    converges. We talked about the specific case of an infinite geometric series, which converges if and only if $|r| < 1$. Another type of series which can be summed is called a "telescoping" series, such as $\sum\limits_{n=1}^{\infty} \left(\frac{1}{n} - \frac{1}{n+1} \right)$. This series converges to 1 because its sequence of partial sums is: $\frac{1}{2}, \frac{2}{3}, \frac{3}{4}, \frac{4}{5}, \ldots$, which clearly converges to 1. To see why such a series is called "telescoping," consider the following:

$$
\sum_{n=1}^{\infty} \left(\frac{1}{n} - \frac{1}{n+1} \right) = \left(1 - \frac{1}{2} \right) + \left(\frac{1}{2} - \frac{1}{3} \right) + \left(\frac{1}{3} - \frac{1}{4} \right) + \ldots = 1.
$$

    The sum collapses, and all terms cancel except the first.

3. What is the Ratio Test? ... Comparison Test? ... Integral Test?

    All of these tests are used to determine if $\sum\limits_{n=1}^{\infty} a_n$ converges.

    Ratio Test: Consider the limit of the absolute value of the ratio of successive terms, that is $\lim\limits_{n\to\infty} \left| \frac{a_{n+1}}{a_n} \right|$. If this limit exists and is less than 1, then the series converges. If this limit exists and is equal to one, then you must use another test because the Ratio Test is inconclusive. In all other cases, the series diverges.

    As an example, let's consider $\sum\limits_{n=1}^{\infty} \frac{2^n}{n!}$. Using the Ratio Test,

$$
\lim_{n\to\infty} \left| \frac{\frac{2^{n+1}}{(n+1)!}}{\frac{2^n}{n!}} \right| = \lim_{n\to\infty} \left| \frac{2^{n+1}}{(n+1)!} \frac{n!}{2^n} \right| = \lim_{n\to\infty} \left| \frac{2}{n+1} \right| = 0 < 1.
$$

    Hence this series converges.

Comparison Test: If you know that $0 \le a_n \le b_n$ for all n and that $\sum_{n=1}^{\infty} b_n$ converges, then you know that $\sum_{n=1}^{\infty} a_n$ also converges (because the a_n sum is smaller than a known convergent series). If on the other hand, you know that $0 \le b_n \le a_n$ for all n and that $\sum_{n=1}^{\infty} b_n$ diverges, then you know that $\sum_{n=1}^{\infty} a_n$ also diverges (because the a_n sum is bigger than a known divergent series).

It helps to have a list of known convergent and known divergent series. We know geometric series converge if and only if $|r| < 1$. Also, the series $\sum_{n=1}^{\infty} \frac{1}{n^p}$ converges if and only if $p > 1$ (which can be proved using the Integral Test, below).

As an example of how to use the Comparison Test, let's consider $\sum_{n=1}^{\infty} \frac{2^n}{3^n + n}$. We first notice that $\frac{2^n}{3^n + n} < \frac{2^n}{3^n} = \left(\frac{2}{3}\right)^n$. Therefore, since $\sum_{n=1}^{\infty} \left(\frac{2}{3}\right)^n$ converges (geometric with $|r| < 1$), then the series $\sum_{n=1}^{\infty} \frac{2^n}{3^n + n}$ converges also.

Integral Test: Suppose that $f(x) \ge 0$ for all $x \ge 1$. Then the Integral Test says that the series $\sum_{n=1}^{\infty} f(n)$ converges if and only if the improper integral $\int_{1}^{\infty} f(x)\,dx$ converges.

As an example, let's look at the series $\sum_{n=1}^{\infty} \frac{1}{n}$. Does this series converge or diverge? The Integral Test says that we can consider the integral $\int_{1}^{\infty} \frac{1}{x}\,dx$.

$$\int_{1}^{\infty} \frac{1}{x}\,dx = \lim_{B \to \infty} \left[\int_{1}^{B} \frac{1}{x}\,dx \right] = \lim_{B \to \infty} \left[\ln x\right]\big|_{1}^{B} = \lim_{B \to \infty} \left[\ln B\right],$$

which does not exist (because it diverges to infinity). Hence the series $\sum_{n=1}^{\infty} \frac{1}{n}$ diverges.

4. Are there any other tests?

There are other tests as well, a few of which are mentioned here.

Test for Divergence: If $\lim_{n \to \infty} a_n \ne 0$, then the series $\sum_{n=1}^{\infty} a_n$ diverges.

Alternating Series Test: If the series $\sum\limits_{n=1}^{\infty} a_n$ is alternating in sign, then it converges if and only if $\lim\limits_{n\to\infty} a_n = 0$.

Root Test: If $\lim\limits_{n\to\infty} \sqrt[n]{|a_n|}$ exists and is less than 1, then the series $\sum\limits_{n=1}^{\infty} a_n$ converges. If the limit is equal to one, then you must use another test because this one is inconclusive. In all other cases, the series diverges.

5. Sample Problems

  (a) Show that the Ratio Test fails for $\sum\limits_{n=1}^{\infty} \dfrac{1}{n}$.

  (b) Which of the following series converge and which diverge? Which tests did you use?

   i. $\sum\limits_{n=1}^{\infty} \dfrac{n+1}{n!}$

   ii. $\sum\limits_{n=1}^{\infty} \dfrac{3^n - 2}{4^n + 2}$

   iii. $\sum\limits_{n=1}^{\infty} \dfrac{1}{n^2}$

   iv. $\sum\limits_{n=1}^{\infty} \dfrac{1}{n^2 + n}$

   v. $\sum\limits_{n=1}^{\infty} \dfrac{1}{\sqrt{n}}$

   vi. $\sum\limits_{n=1}^{\infty} \dfrac{4n^2}{2^n}$

   vii. $\sum\limits_{n=1}^{\infty} \dfrac{n}{n+1}$

   viii. $\sum\limits_{n=1}^{\infty} (-1)^n$

   ix. $\sum\limits_{n=1}^{\infty} 5$

   x. $\sum\limits_{n=2}^{\infty} \dfrac{1}{n^n}$

  (c) If you apply the Ratio Test to a geometric series, what do you obtain? Is this consistent with what we know of geometric series?

6. Answers to Sample Problems

(a) Show that the Ratio Test fails for $\displaystyle\sum_{n=1}^{\infty} \frac{1}{n}$.

$$\lim_{n\to\infty} \left| \frac{\frac{1}{n+1}}{\frac{1}{n}} \right| = \lim_{n\to\infty} \frac{n}{n+1} = 1.$$

Therefore, the Ratio Test is inconclusive.

(b) Which of the following series converge and which diverge? Which tests did you use?

i. $\displaystyle\sum_{n=1}^{\infty} \frac{n+1}{n!}$ converges. Using the Ratio Test,

$$\lim_{n\to\infty} \left| \frac{(n+2)}{(n+1)!} \frac{n!}{(n+1)} \right| = \lim_{n\to\infty} \frac{n+2}{n^2 + 2n + 1} = 0 < 1.$$

ii. $\displaystyle\sum_{n=1}^{\infty} \frac{3^n - 2}{4^n + 2}$ converges. We know that $\frac{3^n - 2}{4^n + 2} < \frac{3^n}{4^n} = \left(\frac{3}{4}\right)^n$, which is a convergent

geometric series. Therefore, the Comparison Test says that $\displaystyle\sum_{n=1}^{\infty} \frac{3^n - 2}{4^n + 2}$ converges.

iii. $\displaystyle\sum_{n=1}^{\infty} \frac{1}{n^2}$ converges. Using the Integral Test,

$$\int_1^\infty \frac{1}{x^2}\, dx = \lim_{B\to\infty} \int_1^B \frac{1}{x^2}\, dx = \lim_{B\to\infty} \left(-\frac{1}{B} + 1 \right) = 1.$$

Because the integral converges, the series also converges. [The Integral Test can also show that $\displaystyle\sum_{n=1}^{\infty} \frac{1}{n^p}$ converges for any $p > 1$.]

iv. $\displaystyle\sum_{n=1}^{\infty} \frac{1}{n^2 + n}$ converges by comparison to the previous problem: $\frac{1}{n^2 + n} < \frac{1}{n^2}$.

v. $\displaystyle\sum_{n=1}^{\infty} \frac{1}{\sqrt{n}}$ diverges. Using the Integral Test,

$$\int_1^\infty \frac{1}{\sqrt{x}}\, dx = \lim_{B\to\infty} \int_1^B \frac{1}{\sqrt{x}}\, dx = \lim_{B\to\infty} 2\sqrt{x}\Big|_1^B = \lim_{B\to\infty} (2\sqrt{B} - 2),$$

which diverges. One could also use the fact that $\displaystyle\sum_{n=1}^{\infty} \frac{1}{n^p}$ diverges if $p \le 1$.

vi. $\displaystyle\sum_{n=1}^{\infty} \frac{4n^2}{2^n}$ converges. Using the Ratio Test,

$$\lim_{n\to\infty} \left| \frac{4(n+1)^2}{2^{n+1}} \frac{2^n}{4n^2} \right| = \frac{1}{2} \lim_{n\to\infty} \frac{4n^2 + 8n + 4}{4n^2} = \frac{1}{2} < 1.$$

vii. $\displaystyle\sum_{n=1}^{\infty} \frac{n}{n+1}$ diverges. Using the Test for Divergence, $\frac{n}{n+1} \to 1$ as $n \to \infty$. Since the size of the terms approaches 1, there is no way for this series to converge.

viii. $\displaystyle\sum_{n=1}^{\infty} (-1)^n$ diverges because the sequence of partial sums: $-1, 0, -1, 0, \ldots$, does not converge.

ix. $\displaystyle\sum_{n=1}^{\infty} 5$ diverges because the sequence of partial sums: $5, 10, 15, \ldots$ does not converge.

x. $\displaystyle\sum_{n=2}^{\infty} \frac{1}{n^n}$ converges by comparison to $\frac{1}{n^2}$. Since $n \geq 2$, $\frac{1}{n^n} \leq \frac{1}{n^2}$. Since the series $\displaystyle\sum_{n=2}^{\infty} \frac{1}{n^2}$ converges, this series converges. [One could also compare this series to $\frac{1}{2^n}$.]

(c) If you apply the Ratio Test to a geometric series, what do you obtain? Is this consistent with what we know of geometric series?

$$\lim_{n \to \infty} \left| \frac{a_1 r^n}{a_1 r^{n-1}} \right| = \lim_{n \to \infty} |r| = |r|.$$

According to the Ratio Test, this series converges if $|r| < 1$, which is consistent with what we know of geometric series.

c. Calculate Taylor series and Taylor polynomials of basic functions

1. What is a Taylor polynomial? How is that different from a Taylor series?

A Taylor polynomial is the best polynomial approximation to a given function near a given point. That means that the degree n Taylor polynomial $P_n(x)$ for $f(x)$ at $x = a$ has the same value and the same first n derivatives as the function does at that point. That is, $P_n(a) = f(a)$, $P_n'(a) = f'(a)$, $P_n''(a) = f''(a)$, $\ldots$, $P_n^{(n)}(a) = f^{(n)}(a)$. The general formula for the degree n Taylor polynomial of $f(x)$ near $x = a$ is:

$$f(a) + f'(a)(x - a) + \frac{f''(a)}{2!}(x-a)^2 + \frac{f'''(a)}{3!}(x-a)^3 + \ldots + \frac{f^{(n)}(a)}{n!}(x-a)^n.$$

When $a = 0$, the formula simplifies to:

$$f(0) + f'(0)x + \frac{f''(0)}{2!}x^2 + \frac{f'''(0)}{3!}x^3 + \ldots + \frac{f^{(n)}(0)}{n!}x^n.$$

A Taylor series is an infinite version of a Taylor polynomial. It has *all* the same derivatives at the point as does the original function. The general formula for the Taylor series for $f(x)$ at (or near) $x = a$ is:

$$f(a) + f'(a)(x - a) + \frac{f''(a)}{2!}(x-a)^2 + \frac{f'''(a)}{3!}(x-a)^3 + \ldots + \frac{f^{(n)}(a)}{n!}(x-a)^n + \ldots.$$

When $a = 0$, the formula simplifies to:

$$f(0) + f'(0)x + \frac{f''(0)}{2!}x^2 + \frac{f'''(0)}{3!}x^3 + \ldots + \frac{f^{(n)}(0)}{n!}x^n + \ldots.$$

2. What are the Taylor series of some basic functions?

Here are some commonly used Taylor series at $x = 0$.

$$e^x = 1 + x + \frac{x^2}{2!} + \frac{x^3}{3!} + \dots$$

$$\sin x = x - \frac{x^3}{3!} + \frac{x^5}{5!} - \frac{x^7}{7!} + \dots$$

$$\cos x = 1 - \frac{x^2}{2!} + \frac{x^4}{4!} - \frac{x^6}{6!} + \dots$$

$$\frac{1}{1-x} = 1 + x + x^2 + x^3 + \dots$$

$$\ln(1+x) = x - \frac{x^2}{2} + \frac{x^3}{3} - \frac{x^4}{4} + \dots$$

$$(1+x)^k = 1 + kx + \frac{k(k-1)}{2!}x^2 + \frac{k(k-1)(k-2)}{3!}x^3 + \dots$$

Each of these Taylor series can be manipulated through substitution, multiplication, differentiation and integration. For example, the Taylor series for e^{-x^2} is the same as the Taylor series of e^x, but with $-x^2$ substituted in place of x:

$$e^{-x^2} = 1 - x^2 + \frac{x^4}{2!} - \frac{x^6}{3!} + \dots.$$

Also

$$\frac{1}{1+x^2} = \frac{1}{1-(-x^2)} = 1 - x^2 + x^4 - x^6 + \dots.$$

These kinds of manipulations work, because $x^2 \to 0$ as $x \to 0$.

3. Sample Problems

   (a) Using Taylor series, show that the derivative of e^x is e^x.

   (b) Using Taylor series, show that the derivative of $\sin x$ is $\cos x$ and that the derivative of $\cos x$ is $-\sin x$.

   (c) Using Taylor series, verify that $\lim\limits_{x \to 0} \dfrac{\sin x}{x} = 1$.

   (d) Using Taylor series, find $\lim\limits_{x \to 0} \dfrac{1 - \cos x}{x^2}$.

   (e) Find Taylor series for $\sin 2x$, $\cos 5x$, and $\ln(1-x)$.

   (f) Using the general formula for a Taylor series at $x = 0$, derive the Taylor series for e^x.

4. Answers to Sample Problems

   (a) Using Taylor series, show that the derivative of e^x is e^x.

$$\frac{d}{dx}e^x = \frac{d}{dx}\left(1 + x + \frac{x^2}{2!} + \frac{x^3}{3!} + \frac{x^4}{4!} + \dots\right)$$

$$= 0 + 1 + \frac{2x}{2!} + \frac{3x^2}{3!} + \frac{4x^3}{4!} + \dots$$

$$= 1 + x + \frac{x^2}{2!} + \frac{x^3}{3!} + \dots = e^x$$

(b) Using Taylor series, show that the derivative of $\sin x$ is $\cos x$ and that the derivative of $\cos x$ is $-\sin x$.

$$\frac{d}{dx}(\sin x) = \frac{d}{dx}\left(x - \frac{x^3}{3!} + \frac{x^5}{5!} - \frac{x^7}{7!} + \ldots\right) = 1 - \frac{x^2}{2!} + \frac{x^4}{4!} - \frac{x^6}{6!} + \ldots = \cos x$$

$$\frac{d}{dx}(\cos x) = \frac{d}{dx}\left(1 - \frac{x^2}{2!} + \frac{x^4}{4!} - \frac{x^6}{6!} + \ldots\right) = 0 - x + \frac{x^3}{3!} - \frac{x^5}{5!} + \ldots = -\sin x$$

(c) Using Taylor series, verify that $\lim\limits_{x\to 0}\dfrac{\sin x}{x} = 1$.

$$\lim_{x\to 0}\frac{\sin x}{x} = \lim_{x\to 0}\frac{x - \frac{x^3}{3!} + \frac{x^5}{5!} - \frac{x^7}{7!} + \ldots}{x} = \lim_{x\to 0}\left(1 - \frac{x^2}{3!} + \frac{x^4}{5!} - \frac{x^6}{7!} + \ldots\right) = 1$$

(d) Using Taylor series, find $\lim\limits_{x\to 0}\dfrac{1 - \cos x}{x^2} \cdot \dfrac{1}{2}$

$$\lim_{x\to 0}\frac{1 - \cos x}{x^2} = \lim_{x\to 0}\frac{1 - \left(1 - \frac{x^2}{2!} + \frac{x^4}{4!} - \frac{x^6}{6!} + \ldots\right)}{x^2} = \lim_{x\to 0}\left(\frac{1}{2} - \frac{x^2}{4!} + \frac{x^4}{6!} - \ldots\right) = \frac{1}{2}$$

(e) Find Taylor series for $\sin 2x$, $\cos 5x$, and $\ln(1 - x)$.

$$\sin 2x = (2x) - \frac{(2x)^3}{3!} + \frac{(2x)^5}{5!} - \frac{(2x)^7}{7!} + \ldots = 2x - \frac{8x^3}{3!} + \frac{32x^5}{5!} - \frac{128x^7}{7!} + \ldots$$

$$\cos 5x = 1 - \frac{25x^2}{2!} + \frac{625x^4}{4!} - \frac{15{,}625x^6}{6!} + \ldots$$

$$\ln(1 - x) = \ln(1 + (-x)) = -x - \frac{x^2}{2} - \frac{x^3}{3} - \frac{x^4}{4} - \ldots$$

(f) Using the general formula for a Taylor series at $x = 0$, derive the Taylor series for e^x. Since every derivative of e^x is equal to e^x, $f(0) = f'(0) = \ldots = f^{(n)}(0) = e^0 = 1$. So the Taylor series for e^x is

$$1 + x + \frac{x^2}{2!} + \frac{x^3}{3!} + \ldots + \frac{x^n}{n!} + \ldots.$$

Made in the USA
San Bernardino, CA
13 March 2019